Items should be returned on or before the last date shown below. Items not already requested by other borrowers may be renewed in person, in writing or by telephone. To renew, please quote the number on the barcode label. To renew online a PIN is required. This can be requested at your local library.
Renew online @ **www.dublincitypubliclibraries.ie**
Fines charged for overdue items will include postage incurred in recovery. Damage to or loss of items will be charged to the borrower.

Leabharlanna Poiblí Chathair Bhaile Átha Cliath
Dublin City Public Libraries

Baile Átha Cliath
Dublin City

Brainse Mheal Ráthluirc
Charleville Mall Branch
Tel. 8749619

Date Due	Date Due	Date Due

WITHDRAWN FROM STOCK
DUBLIN CITY PUBLIC LIBRARIES

D0411005

Detox in a weekend

an easy-to-follow diet and health plan

Lose weight and improve your well-being with a unique cleansing routine

50 tempting, healthy recipes shown step by step in more than 275 beautiful photographs, with nutritional information throughout

Contributing Editor Maggie Pannell

LORENZ BOOKS

NOTES

Bracketed terms are intended for American readers.

For all recipes, quantities are given in both metric and imperial measures and, where appropriate, in standard cups and spoons. Follow one set, but not a mixture, because they are not interchangeable.

Standard spoon and cup measures are level. 1 tsp = 5ml, 1 tbsp = 15ml, 1 cup = 250ml/8fl oz.

Australian standard tablespoons are 20ml. Australian readers should use 3 tsp in place of 1 tbsp for measuring small quantities of gelatine, flour, salt, etc.

American pints are 16fl oz/2 cups. American readers should use 20fl oz/ 2.5 cups in place of 1 pint when measuring liquids.

Electric oven temperatures in this book are for conventional ovens. When using a fan oven, the temperature will probably need to be reduced by about 10–20°C/ 20–40°F. Since ovens vary, you should check with your manufacturer's instruction book for guidance.

The nutritional analysis given for each recipe is calculated per portion (i.e. serving or item), unless otherwise stated. If the recipe gives a range, such as Serves 4–6, then the nutritional analysis will be for the smaller portion size, i.e. 6 servings. Measurements for sodium do not include salt added to taste.

Medium (US large) eggs are used unless otherwise stated.

The diets and information in this book are not intended to replace advice from a qualified practitioner, doctor or dietician. Always consult your health practitioner before adopting any of the suggestions in this book. Neither the author nor the publisher can accept any liability for failure to follow this advice. A detox diet is not recommended for children, the elderly or pregnant women.

This edition is published by Lorenz Books, an imprint of Anness Publishing Ltd, 108 Great Russell Street, London WC1B 3NA; info@anness.com

www.lorenzbooks.com; www.annesspublishing.com

If you like the images in this book and would like to investigate using them for publishing, promotions or advertising, please visit our website www.practicalpictures.com for more information.

© Anness Publishing Ltd 2015

All rights reserved. No part of this publication may be reproduced, stored in a retrieval system, or transmitted in any way or by any means, electronic, mechanical, photocopying, recording or otherwise, without the prior written permission of the copyright holder.

A CIP catalogue record for this book is available from the British Library.

Publisher: Joanna Lorenz
Project Editor: Lucy Doncaster
Designer: Nigel Partridge
Production Controller: Pirong Wang

PUBLISHER'S NOTE
Although the advice and information in this book are believed to be accurate and true at the time of going to press, neither the authors nor the publisher can accept any legal responsibility or liability for any errors or omissions that may have been made nor for any inaccuracies nor for any loss, harm or injury that comes about from following instructions or advice in this book.

CONTENTS

Introduction

Detox diets have become increasingly popular and no wonder, as they offer fantastic health benefits, claiming to leave you feeling relaxed, refreshed and rejuvenated. In an increasingly toxic world, a detox programme can help your body's in-built detoxifiers to counter the effects of pollution and the many potentially harmful, chemical substances with a spring-clean that leaves you looking and feeling brighter and healthier.

What is detoxing?

Detoxing is an ancient therapy that has been practised in various forms for hundreds of years. It is believed to cleanse the digestive system and help the body eliminate waste products and various toxins absorbed from the air, soil, water and food, as well as toxic substances produced by the body itself. Although this has not been medically or scientifically proven, a detox diet offers many health benefits and is useful for giving the body's own detoxification system a helping hand occasionally, especially since the body has to deal with an ever-increasing toxic load in the modern world.

Detox diets, although based on the same idea, vary in the length of time they're recommended for and the foods that are allowed or avoided. Strict detox diets allow just fruit and vegetables, ideally raw and often taken as juices,

Below: Raw vegetables are key detox foods, so eat them in abundance.

with plenty of water for just one or two days. This is a light fasting regime, designed to give the body's digestive system a rest, and it should not be continued for a longer period. A less restrictive regime is based on eating healthy meals, consisting of plenty of fruit and vegetables, home-made soups, whole grains, beans, peas, lentils, fish, skinless poultry, seeds and nuts. Wheat and dairy products, caffeine drinks and alcohol, are not allowed on either plans.

The detox diet regime should also be combined with regular exercise and complementary therapies, including pampering beauty treatments and relaxing techniques, in order to gain the full holistic benefit.

Above: Drinking plenty of water is essential for health at all times.

Benefits

A detox programme can improve your digestion, boost your immune system and give you a renewed zest for life. Benefits may include better sleep, improved hair, nails and skin, more energy, stress relief, weight loss and possibly even the reduction of cellulite. This is achieved by restricting the intake of toxins and chemical substances, eating a healthy diet and including regular exercise, all of which have the combined effect of making you feel and look better and adopt a positive attitude towards your health.

WHO SHOULDN'T DETOX?

Don't embark on a detox if any of the following apply to you:

- If you are pregnant, trying to fall pregnant or breast–feeding.
- If you are diabetic or following a special diet for another condition.
- If you have recently been ill or are recovering from an illness. Wait until you feel completely better.
- If you are under 18 years of age, or over 65 years of age.
- If you are taking any kind of medication, in which case you must first consult your doctor.

Is it for you?

The checklist on the right of this page will tell you if you could be suffering from toxic overload. If you have ticked at least five of the questions, you are likely to be feeling below par and could benefit from a detox.

As long as you are fit and healthy, it is likely to be safe for you to follow a detox programme. However, you must first check with your doctor, especially if you suffer from any health conditions or are taking any medication. Do not attempt to self-diagnose any symptoms that may have an underlying physical cause and require medical investigation.

Remember that a detox diet is not designed to be a weight-reducing diet, nor is it an elimination diet for identifying the cause of food allergies, although it may be successful in helping with weight loss or spotlighting a food sensitivity. For successful, long-term weight loss, a healthy balanced diet combined with regular exercise is essential.

Once you've completed your detox, gradually reintroduce food and drinks that were restricted, but avoid junk foods, which are high in fat and sugar and with poor nutritional value. Maintain and build on the benefits gained by following the basic principles of leading a healthy lifestyle.

Right: Frequent headaches can be a symptom of toxic overload.

Timing

You can detox at any time of the year, although popular times tend to be at the start of spring or summer, after the Christmas and New Year excesses, or in preparation for a holiday or a special occasion. There is nothing like a big incentive to spur you on, but the most important factor is to start with a positive attitude.

Choose a time when you are not too busy and can allow yourself plenty of time to relax. Delegate as many tasks as you can to others so that you do not feel pressured. A short weekend detox should be relatively easy to plan, but you should make sure there are no important dates like dinner parties or holidays that could make it difficult to stick to a prescribed eating plan.

It is also not a good time to detox if you are going through any kind of particularly stressful major life change, such as moving house, changing your job, or divorce or separation. Wait until your life is calmer, when a detox may be just what you need for a new lease of life following a particularly demanding or worrying occasion or point in time.

Beyond detox

For the long-term, a detox should be followed by choosing a healthy balanced diet, including a wide variety of foods from each of the different food groups. This can aid in the prevention of chronic illnesses, such as cancer and heart disease.

ARE YOU SUFFERING FROM TOXIN OVERLOAD?

Check how toxic you are by answering the questions below. The more questions that you answer 'yes' to, the more toxic you are likely to be and the more likely you are to benefit from a detox.

1   Are you constantly tired and lethargic?
2   Do you have difficulty getting a good night's sleep?
3   Do you suffer from frequent headaches or migraine attacks?
4   Do you suffer from bloating and wind?
5   Do you suffer from constipation or diarrhoea?
6   Do you suffer from catarrh and sinus problems?
7   Do you have difficulty maintaining concentration?
8   Do you suffer from frequent mood swings, anxiety or bouts of depression?
9   Do you frequently feel stressed and irritable?
10 Is your skin spotty or dull, or do you suffer from skin problems, such as eczema, dermatitis or psoriasis?
11 Is your hair dull and lifeless?
12 Do you sometimes have aches and pains in your joints?
13 Do you suffer from frequent colds and other minor illnesses?
14 Do you smoke, live with a smoker, or work in a smoky environment?
15 Do you drink alcohol heavily or regularly?
16 Do you drink more than 3–4 cups of coffee, tea or cola drinks daily?
17 Are you addicted to chocolate?
18 Do you crave sugary and snack foods?
19 Is your diet high in processed foods and convenience meals?
20 Have you developed any food sensitivities?

the
detox
diet

Discover how to detox your body and mind safely
and efficiently through healthy eating combined
with exercise and relaxing complementary
therapies. All aspects of the diet are discussed,
including information on where toxins come from,
food sensitivities, nutritional information and what
the benefits of a detox are.

What are toxins and where do they come from?

An overload of toxins can be responsible for causing a range of health problems. So what are the different toxins that we are now exposed to in the modern industrial world and what can we do to restrict our exposure?

What are toxins?

Toxins are potentially harmful substances that pollute and irritate our bodies, putting a strain on the efficiency of our vital organs. There are many different kinds of toxins and they are nothing new, but we are now living in an increasingly toxic world, due to modern technology, intensive farming and food production methods, and a greater use of chemicals, all of which may affect our health and well-being.

Although the human body is designed to deal with these unwanted substances, a build-up of toxins puts an extra strain on our natural detoxifying system, especially with increasing age. This can lead to troublesome symptoms and health conditions,

Below: Traffic exhaust fumes are a major air pollutant.

particularly affecting the digestive and respiratory systems. Asthma, for example, is becoming increasingly common, and although environmental pollution is not necessarily the cause, it is certainly a contributing factor and can be responsible for making the symptoms worse. Increasing evidence and scientific research now suggest that many health conditions and chronic diseases may be linked to toxins in our world and lifestyle.

Where do toxins come from?

Toxins bombard us every day. Not only are they produced naturally in the body, but they can enter the body in the air we breathe, from pollutants in the atmosphere and our environment, and in the food, drinks, drugs and medicines that we consume. Toxic chemical substances are also absorbed through the skin from cosmetics, toiletries and household products, including everyday materials such as paint, glue and electrical products. In fact, unless you live in a sterile bubble, it is impossible to avoid everyday exposure to toxins.

Environment

Pollutants in the air include car exhaust fumes, cigarette smoke, fumes from industrial waste, air-conditioning and heating systems, cleaning fluids, air fresheners, paints, detergents, deodorants and hairsprays.

Tap water

Water quality regulations are imposed to ensure that tap water is safe to drink. It also contains valuable minerals, depending on the source and region. However, there is increasing concern about levels of pollutants, including nitrates from fertilizers, weedkillers, industrial chemicals, poisonous metals (such as lead and mercury) and oestrogen-like chemicals, that may be present (albeit in minute quantities) and their possible effect on our health. You can easily find out about the quality of water in your area. If you are concerned, buy a water filter or choose bottled water.

Chemical residues

Agricultural land is treated with fertilizers, crops are sprayed with pesticides and growth regulators, and animals and farmed fish may be fed antibiotics. All of these practices can leave artificial chemical residues either on or in our food, as well as contaminating the environment and water supplies. Increasing concern about these pollutants and a desire to move towards a greener future has led to more and more farms converting to an organic system and more people choosing organic foods.

Free radicals

The body constantly makes and breaks down free radicals, and in small amounts they are helpful as a natural defence against invading bacteria and viruses. However, certain factors such as cigarette smoke, environmental pollution and over-exposure to sunlight,

can accelerate their production. In large amounts, they are thought to cause damage to cell walls and DNA (the genetic material found in cells), speeding up the ageing process and contributing to the development of heart disease and some cancers. Antioxidant enzymes and nutrients in the blood (produced naturally and ingested in food) help to neutralize and deactivate free radicals and render them harmless.

Food additives

Due to a diet that tends to be largely made up of processed foods, manufactured to suit a modern lifestyle, where speed and convenience are often key to the choices we make, much of our food now contains a wide array of additives. Preservatives are added to prevent the food spoiling, to protect against contamination and to increase the shelf life; emulsifiers improve the texture and consistency of foods; colours, flavourings, flavour enhancers and sweeteners are used to alter the appearance or taste of a food or drink, and various other additives may be used for miscellaneous purposes such as for glazing or as anti-foaming agents.

All these additives would not be necessary if we chose to eat more fresh food that was seasonal and produced locally. Although only some people may be particularly sensitive to certain additives, the combined effect adds up to a considerable intake, which may take its toll on our bodies in ways that are not yet fully understood.

Above: Organic farming avoids the use of chemical fertilizers and pesticides.

Alcohol

Drinking alcohol in moderation is relaxing and sociable and can be positively good for your health, but alcohol is basically a poison to the body and puts strain on the liver. Alcoholic drinks, such as wine, beer, cider and alcopops, may also contain chemical additives such as sulphite preservatives that some people can be allergic to. Sulphites can trigger an asthma attack in susceptible individuals.

Cigarettes

Tobacco smoke, which is inhaled into the lungs, contains nicotine and tar as well as many other chemical substances. Not only is the nicotine extremely addictive, but the smoke exposes the body to powerful and harmful chemical compounds that are known to cause cancer and other tobacco-related diseases, such as heart disease and bronchitis.

Left: Highly processed convenience foods are loaded with additives.

HOW TO RESTRICT EXPOSURE TO TOXINS

• Avoid smoky environments and if you're a smoker, seek help and advice on how to kick the habit.
• Avoid walking in built-up areas, close to traffic or in industrial areas.
• If you live in a town or city, try to escape to the seaside or country as often as you can for fresh air.
• Wear a mask if you cycle in heavy traffic conditions.
• Cut down on or cease using unnecessary household chemical products, such as aerosol air fresheners.
• Buy eco-friendly household cleaners, washing powder and washing-up liquid.
• Choose organic produce whenever possible.
• Adopt a 'greener' lifestyle.

Leabharlanna Poiblí Chathair Bhaile Átha Cliath
Dublin City Public Libraries

How diet affects health

Diet is a complex affair. Just think about all the foods you have eaten over the past few days and imagine how their substance and value may affect your body. Then consider all the other factors in your life that may influence your health and you can begin to see why it is generally so difficult to identify the causes of troublesome symptoms and conditions.

Diet in general, or a particular food or group of foods may well be at the root of the problem, but it's important to consider and examine a broad view of possibilities before eliminating foods indiscriminately from your diet.

Symptoms may be attributable to other medical conditions so it's vital to always check with your doctor in the first instance to safely rule out any possible underlying physical causes.

Below: Wheat products can cause gastrointestinal complaints.

Above: Always discuss troublesome symptoms with your doctor.

Digestive problems

Wheat and dairy products are frequently suspected and sometimes identified as causing bloating, abdominal pain and wind in susceptible individuals. Symptoms of a digestive disorder may also include diarrhoea and constipation. This may be due to a true allergy or an intolerance. The degree of sensitivity may be slight, moderate or severe and there may also be other symptoms present, such as asthma, eczema, rashes and wheezing. Food intolerance or a food allergy, however mild it may seem, should always be taken seriously, so seeking professional diagnosis is very important.

Could also be due to:

• Irritable bowel syndrome (IBS). This is the most common bowel disorder in the Western world although sufferers are often too embarrassed to discuss the condition with their doctor. It is twice as common in women as in men and is most likely to affect people between the ages of 20 and 40 years. Typical symptoms include stomach-ache, bloating and wind, as well as constipation and/or diarrhoea. The condition may be triggered by stress, a hormone imbalance or different types of food. Wheat (especially bran), beans, peas, lentils and dairy products are common food culprits.

There is no single effective treatment, but a dietician will often recommend a special diet that may exclude suspected offending foods. If you think that you may be suffering from this condition, keep a food diary together with a record of your symptoms and consult your doctor for referral to a dietician.

• Coeliac disease. This life-long inflammatory condition is caused by a permanent adverse reaction to gluten, a protein in wheat, as well as other similar proteins in rye, barley and oats. Diarrhoea, abdominal pain and wind are common symptoms and adults may find that they lose weight and become anaemic. Coeliac disease used to be rare, but more and more doctors are beginning to recognize the disorder. The average incidence in the West is 1 in 100 people and about one in 1000–1500 people are affected worldwide. Once diagnosed, the condition can be controlled by following a strict gluten-free diet for life, under the guidance of a dietician. There is now a wide variety of gluten-free foods readily available, allowing you to have a less limited diet.

Above: Dairy products could be responsible for sinus problems.

Respiratory problems

Dairy products can lead to excess mucus in the sinuses and nasal passages, so if you suffer from a persistent stuffy or runny nose (perennial rhinitis) or congested sinuses (sinusitis), dairy foods could be the culprit. A short detox, eliminating all dairy products from your diet, will help to highlight if this could be the cause of your symptoms.

Could also be due to: An allergic reaction to any substance that may trigger an individual reaction. This could be a food or an additive in the food, or it could be a household or cosmetic product or something in the environment that the body regards as alien and potentially harmful. House-dust mites, pollen, feathers, animal fur, air fresheners and washing powders may all be offending triggers. Allergic reactions can be responsible for triggering asthma attacks, so it is important to always seek medical advice. Some asthmatics are sensitive to sulphite preservatives, commonly used in beer, wine and cider. Labelling laws now require alcoholic drinks to be labelled if they contain sulphites.

Food cravings and addictions

The body can get hooked on certain foods that are eaten frequently and suffer withdrawal symptoms when they are not eaten. This can be caused by foods believed to boost serotonin and endorphin levels in the brain, which provide a feel-good effect, or by sugary foods that give an instant, but temporary blood-sugar fix. Addiction to caffeine is also common. Symptoms include fatigue and mood swings and binging on the culprit food, which can then cause weight gain and bad skin. In effect you can find yourself trapped in an addictive cycle of craving and withdrawal. Refined and sugary foods tend to be responsible, including cereals, cakes, biscuits, chocolate and sugar as well as tea and coffee. Sometimes a food craving can indicate a sensitivity to it, and this should be investigated by a dietician or a professional allergy specialist.

Skin problems

Common complaints include rashes, eczema and spots, and although acne is generally a teenage problem, it can strike as late as middle-age. Eczema, characterized by red, itchy, dry and flaky skin that may bleed or blister, is often brought on by allergens. This may be an external irritant, such as wool, metal or a detergent, to which the skin is sensitive, or a reaction to something eaten. Milk, eggs, fish, shellfish, tomatoes, nuts and wheat are

Above: Eggs may be a problem food and exacerbate eczema.

common culprits. A medically supervised exclusion diet can identify the offending trigger, if symptoms improve or disappear when a suspect food is avoided. Drinking plenty of water daily will help improve the general condition of the skin by flushing out the body's waste products.

Could also be due to:
• Emotional stress.
• Hormonal fluctuations, especially in the week before a menstrual period.
• Nutrient deficiencies.

Right: Chocolate is a common food addiction.

Left: Drinking a cup of hot water with a generous squeeze of lemon juice in the morning will stimulate the liver and the gall bladder to kickstart the process of detoxing the body.

Headaches

These may be triggered by a food sensitivity, additives used in certain processed foods, or by consuming excessive amounts of caffeine, which alters the blood supply to the brain. Chocolate, cheese, citrus fruits and alcohol, especially red wine and port, are also commonly cited dietary culprits associated with migraine attacks. Headaches may also be due to an irregular eating pattern. Skipping meals causes blood sugar to plummet, which in turn can precipitate a headache. Try eating regular light meals, do not skip breakfast and if you often wake up with a headache, have a light snack before bedtime to prevent blood sugar levels from dropping too low overnight.

Dehydration can also trigger headaches so be sure to drink plenty of water, especially during hot weather spells, or following strenuous exercise or excessive alcohol consumption.

Could also be due to:
- Poor posture.
- Eye strain.
- Hormonal fluctuations.
- Stress and tension.
- Nasal congestion.
- High blood pressure.
- Poor liver or kidney function.

HEADACHES
Frequent or severe headaches should always be investigated by a medical professional to establish their cause, especially if ordinary painkillers do not help and certainly if you experience other symptoms such as blurred vision, muscle weakness, weight loss or vomiting.

Below: Frequent or severe headaches could be due to a toxic overload, and may be alleviated by making simple changes to the diet.

Tiredness and lack of energy

Sweet snacks, caffeine, alcohol and chocolate can all play havoc with your energy levels, giving you a quick energy boost followed by a rapid fall in sugar levels and an energy dive. Drowsiness may also sometimes be due to a food intolerance. While it is normal to feel sleepy after a big meal, constant lethargy is not normal, and may be due to a sensitivity to grains – particularly wheat, as the process of digestion may induce excessive sleepiness in susceptible individuals.

Could also be due to:
- Coeliac disease.
- Anaemia resulting from poor iron and folic acid absorption.
- An underactive thyroid or a viral infection.
- Stress in your professional and/or personal life.
- Mild dehydration resulting from insufficient fluid intake.
- Diabetes.

Mood swings and depression

There are many reasons for changing moods, and ups and downs are part of everyday life. It may be because you are unhappy, under pressure or worried. Stress makes you feel depressed and may be accompanied by various aches and pains. Over a long time, stress can lead to serious illness, including high blood pressure and heart disease. Identify the root cause and think of ways to cope and reduce the strain.

Everyday foods can affect your mood and nutritional deficiencies, food intolerances and the level of blood sugar in the bloodstream can all influence your mental state. Regular meals, eating foods rich in B vitamins (which are good for the nervous system) and cutting down on caffeine and alcohol will all help to maintain a steady blood sugar level.

Could also be due to:
• Premenstrual syndrome (PMS).
• Clinical depression.

Below: Close contact with a loved one provides comfort when you are down.

Above: Snack on fresh fruit rather than processed foods when you are hungry.

Premenstrual syndrome (PMS)

This is a common female complaint brought on by fluctuating hormone levels, which can be responsible for causing bloating, headaches, breast pain and depression. Research shows that nutrition can influence hormone production, so a change of diet may help to relieve symptoms. Cutting down on saturated fats may relieve breast tenderness and lowering the intake of salt can reduce bloating and water retention. Also avoid coffee and alcohol for 1–2 weeks before a period is due. Small frequent meals, including nutritious snacks, such as fruit, nuts and seeds, will maintain blood sugar levels. Obesity can affect hormone balance so try to keep your weight within acceptable limits. Regular exercise helps to relieve symptoms.

Joint pains

An allergy or intolerance to particular foods could be a contributing factor to joint pain. Pinpointing the culprit foods can be difficult, but common suspects include dairy products, eggs and cereals. An exclusion diet, followed under medical supervision, will help to identify problem foods. Scientific evidence suggests that a diet deficient in antioxidants, particularly vitamins A, C and E and the mineral selenium, may also predispose some people to joint problems. To increase your intake of these nutrients, you should eat a healthy balanced diet, rich in oily fish and shellfish, fresh fruit and vegetables, wholegrain cereals, eggs, nuts and seeds.

Could also be due to:
• Excessive body weight. Not only can this be a cause of joint problems, particularly affecting the hips and knees, but carrying excess weight can add to the pain caused by other factors.
• Lack of exercise. Regular exercise helps to strengthen the muscles responsible for protecting the joints and helps to prevent stiffness.
• Injury or over-exertion. Cut back your exercise routine or change to a less physically demanding activity.

Food allergy and intolerance

Allergies and intolerances are becoming increasingly common and it has been estimated that around 25 per cent of the population may suffer from a sensitivity at some point in their lives. This appears to be a consequence of a number of factors, including increased air pollution, greater use of chemicals, modern living conditions, over-use of antibiotics and other drugs and more stressful lives, all of which weaken the immune system and make us more vulnerable. The potential causes of allergy or intolerance are numerous and can be difficult to identify. Pollen, house-dust mites, pet hair, insect stings and chemicals, as well as food and drink, can trigger an adverse reaction in susceptible individuals.

What's the difference between allergy and intolerance?

These two terms are frequently confused. The main difference between them is that an allergy involves a reaction by the body's immune system, whereas an intolerance does not. Only a small percentage of individuals with sensitivities are truly allergic. Allergies have a genetic link and are more likely to occur in families where there is a history of allergic conditions, including asthma, hay fever and eczema. Allergies and intolerances can occur at any age and stress can be a trigger.

Above: Shellfish can sometimes trigger an allergic reaction.

Food allergy

This is an extreme immune (defence) system response to a food that the body mistakenly believes to be harmful, causing the production of antibodies. This triggers the release of powerful irritating chemicals, such as histamine, into the bloodstream which cause inflammation and symptoms such as vomiting, diarrhoea, skin rashes, oral and facial swelling, breathing difficulties and plummeting blood pressure. Reactions in some cases can be so severe that they may be life threatening. This is known as anaphylactic shock and requires immediate medical attention.

Food intolerance

This may result from a number of different conditions, such as a lack of a digestive enzyme or a damaged intestine (known as leaky gut). Symptoms may be delayed, so it can be difficult to identify the culprit, and are generally not as severe as those experienced with an allergic reaction. They can include bloating, indigestion, migraines, rashes, joint pains and fatigue. It is important to remember that these symptoms may be associated with other conditions so always seek medical advice.

MEDICAL DIAGNOSIS

Following a detox diet may help to relieve symptoms and to identify a problem food, but it should not be used to self-diagnose. Allergic reactions, however mild, need to be taken seriously and professional medical diagnosis is essential. If you think you have a food allergy or intolerance, consult your family doctor. Blood and skin prick tests can be reliable for identifying 'classic' allergies, or an exclusion diet may be recommended in which suspect foods are systematically eliminated from your diet, then reintroduced to see if the symptoms return.

Above: Wheat, nuts and dairy products are some of the foods that can cause sensitivity in susceptible individuals.

Which foods can cause problems?

No food is harmful in itself, but those that are known to cause the greatest percentage of reactions in susceptible people are milk and dairy products, gluten (sometimes just wheat), eggs, fish and shellfish, nuts and soya. Food additives, such as sulphites and benzoates (both used as preservatives) and colourings, may also be culprits.

Gluten

This protein is found in wheat and rye and is related to similar proteins found in rye, barley and oats. People who experience a permanent adverse reaction to gluten are diagnosed as having coeliac disease. This occurs in genetically susceptible individuals and is a lifelong condition. In a coeliac, gluten damages the lining of the small intestine which greatly reduces the ability of the gut to absorb adequate nutrients from food. Coeliac patients may be severely ill with weight loss, vomiting and diarrhoea or they may have chronic, almost trivial symptoms, such as tiredness, lethargy and breathlessness. Adults may have a history of abdominal pain and intestinal upsets, or they may suddenly develop the condition at any time. Anaemia and mouth ulcers, resulting from nutrient deficiencies are also common features. If these symptoms are evident always seek medical advice and do not attempt to self-diagnose. Another possible side effect of intestinal damage is an increased sensitivity to other foods such as soya or lactose in milk.

If coeliac disease is diagnosed, it means cutting out all wheat-based foods including bread, flour, wheat pasta, semolina, couscous, bulghur wheat and certain breakfast cereals as well as cakes, biscuits, pastries and puddings and any processed foods that may include wheat, such as soups, sauces, sausages and stuffing mixes. You will also need to avoid rye and barley (beer, stout and malted drinks) and possibly oats, although a moderate amount can usually be tolerated as they contain less gluten. A gluten-free diet should include plenty of potatoes, rice, beans, peas, lentils, corn and nuts to replace the prohibited foods.

Below: Dairy products can cause an adverse reaction in some people.

Wheat

Many people are intolerant to the whole wheat grain, including wheat starch. Symptoms include bloating, indigestion, lethargy, asthma and skin disorders. Sufferers need to follow a completely wheat-free diet, including many gluten-free products, such as gluten-free bread, which may contain wheat starch. However, other types of cereal such as oats, rye, barley, rice and corn may be included in the diet.

Milk

Lactose intolerance A lack of the enzyme lactase results in an inability to digest lactose, the sugar in milk. Symptoms may include bloating, abdominal pain, wind and diarrhoea. Hard cheese (which is very low in lactose) and yogurt, especially probiotic yogurt (as the bacteria help to digest the lactose), are usually well tolerated. Nut, rice or soya 'milks' or special lactose-reduced milk provide good alternatives, although research suggests that the best way of dealing with the problem is not to avoid lactose-containing foods and potentially risk low calcium intake, but to stabilize symptoms by including small amounts of dairy foods.

Lactose intolerance is usually genetically inherited and is more common among non-white races. It is a relatively common complaint.

Milk allergy Some people have trouble with milk-based products because they cannot tolerate certain milk proteins and the human immune system reacts adversely to them. Symptoms can include eczema, rashes, digestive problems, wheezing, stuffy nose and runny eyes and in rare cases, anaphylactic shock. Generally, all dairy products need to be avoided, including butter, cheese, yogurt and cream and also products with a milk content. Soya, rice and oat 'milks' can be used as alternatives to cow's milk. (These are not suitable for babies under 12 months.) Ideally they should be fortified with calcium and vitamins to ensure an adequate intake of these essential nutrients.

Nuts

Allergies to nuts can develop at any age and are usually life-long. Peanuts are the most likely offender, but other varieties may also cause a reaction. It is essential to avoid all contact with the nuts concerned as a reaction can be very serious. In severe allergy, even slight contact from nut dust in the air may trigger anaphylactic shock, which can be fatal. Nut-allergy sufferers should carry an epi-pen containing adrenaline to counteract a nut reaction if triggered. People with nut allergy may be more prone to anaphylactic reactions if they have asthma or at times of stress.

Eggs

Symptoms of an allergy to eggs may include skin rashes, swelling and stomach upsets as well as asthma and eczema. It is usually the egg white (protein) that causes a problem, but if you are allergic then all eggs and egg products should be avoided, including mayonnaise, cakes, desserts, mousses, meringues and quiches. A powdered, dry egg substitute can be bought from many health food stores.

Benefits of a detox

The benefits you will enjoy from following a detox programme will vary depending on the length and strictness of the regime, the degree of change to your usual lifestyle and eating habits, and your current state of health and well-being. Benefits vary from person to person, but these are the main physical and mental improvements frequently experienced.

Better health
As well as helping to relieve bothersome ailments like headaches and bloating that may be due to food intolerances, a detox diet including plenty of vitamin C from fruit and vegetables can also help to boost your immune system and fight off minor infections – or at least reduce their severity. Including a wide and plentiful variety of fruit and vegetables, packed with antioxidant vitamins and minerals,

Below: Regular exercise, especially when taken in the fresh air, helps to promote mental and physical health.

and other valuable compounds called phytochemicals, also helps to protect against chronic diseases such as heart disease and cancer. Regular consumption of low-fat probiotic yogurt also tops up the good bacteria in the gut, which improves the digestion and helps to relieve disorders such as IBS and constipation, and strengthen the immune system.

Improved appearance
A diet that is rich in vitamins and minerals, with plenty of fruit and vegetables, and that avoids alcohol and cigarettes, will improve the condition of your skin, hair and nails and can help to slow down the ageing process. Fruit and vegetables provide a rich source of vitamin C, needed for the production of collagen (a protein needed for healthy skin, teeth and gums) and also betacarotene, which helps to generate new cells. Overall skin health also depends on proper hydration, so drinking plenty of water helps to promote clearer skin. Regular exercise,

especially if taken in the fresh air, boosts the circulation, delivering oxygen to all body cells, and giving the complexion a healthy glow. Teeth will look brighter if not discoloured by tannins present in red wine and black tea.

Improved mood and inner calm
By choosing nutrient-rich foods, your body is better equipped for coping with stress. You will feel calmer and more relaxed and better able to concentrate and think clearly. Regulating blood sugar levels will help you to avoid mood swings, and a break from alcohol will prevent the depressive effect that dulls the brain and affects the memory.

WComplementary therapies, such as visualization and meditation, are excellent for helping to declutter the mind and induce a relaxed sense of well-being. Feeling happy, optimistic and having a positive outlook on life all help to boost your confidence and self-esteem and promote good health, and a long life span.

Above: A detox diet will help you to sleep better.

naturopaths and beauticians claim that a diet high in processed and refined foods and low in fruit and vegetables can be to blame for causing cellulite. Certainly a low-fat diet that includes plenty of fruit and vegetables may help to reduce it, and regular exercise will definitely help too. Dry skin brushing and massage treatments can also help to improve the appearance of cellulite.

Improved long-term diet

Although certain foods and drinks are restricted temporarily while following a detox programme, the basic principles of the diet should help you to kick bad habits and adopt a pattern of healthy eating that you will be able to maintain afterwards. It is important to remember that a restrictive diet is not recommended as a continued or long-term eating plan.

Restful sleep

Alcohol, cigarettes and caffeine drinks all interfere with sleep patterns and can cause insomnia. As these should all be eliminated during your detox, you will begin to have a better night's sleep. Also, you will not be eating highly processed junk foods that tend to be high in fat and difficult to digest, especially if they are eaten late at night. Regular exercise and many of the complementary and relaxation therapies, chamomile or valerian tea, all of which are recommended while detoxing, will also help you to sleep.

Increased energy

Fatigue can be made worse by not eating the right foods and therefore not getting enough nutrients to promote sustained energy and vitality. Maintaining good nutrition by eating a wide variety of foods, combined with more sleep and a better ability to cope with stress through complementary relaxation techniques, will all help to banish tiredness and replenish your energy levels.

Weight loss

A detox is not designed to be a weight-reducing diet. However, because you are choosing healthy foods (whole grains, low-fat protein foods and plenty of fruit and vegetables), and cutting out foods that are high in fat and sugar, as well as alcohol, you will naturally consume fewer calories and are therefore likely to lose some weight. Also, gentle but regular exercise will encourage weight loss as well as improving muscle tone.

Reduction of cellulite

Some women also notice a reduction in the appearance of cellulite, although there's no sound scientific evidence to support the claim that cellulite is actually caused by a build up of toxins, and therefore by following a detox diet the appearance of cellulite can be reduced or removed. Cellulite has a dimpled, orange-peel-like appearance on the skin and can affect women's thighs, buttocks and upper arms – even if you are slim. The female hormone oestrogen is responsible for women acquiring fat in these areas, and because it is stored just under the skin, it can affect its appearance. Many

Below: A slimmer, more toned figure results from cutting out foods that are high in fat and sugar.

The body's natural detoxifiers

The body is a remarkable system of organic engineering, working to eliminate undesirable substances via the liver, kidneys, lungs, skin, and digestive and lymphatic systems. Generally toxins are dealt with and cleared out routinely and efficiently, but a detox 'spring clean' provides the body with extra help in coping with an increased toxic load.

The digestive system

Your health is often governed by your digestive system. Everything you eat travels from the stomach to the intestines where nutrients are absorbed and waste is eliminated via the bowel. Food is broken down by digestive enzymes and 'friendly' bacteria in the gut. If these are out of sync, due to poor diet, stress, over-use of antibiotics, food intolerances or toxin overload, food remains semi-digested and problems such as constipation, leaky gut, irritable bowel syndrome (IBS), nausea and bloating arise. Food itself can also become toxic if not digested properly.

The liver

This is the most complex human organ and it is responsible for handling almost everything that enters the body. It has hundreds of functions including the removal of toxins from the bloodstream. It is the body's main detoxifier, removing and neutralizing poisons, drugs, alcohol and nicotine. Once made 'safe', these substances can then be eliminated from the body via the kidneys, lungs and bowel. The liver also converts the energy from food into the metabolic nutrients that are needed for cells to function efficiently.

Optimum health depends on the efficient functioning of the liver. If it becomes overloaded with toxins, these are not eliminated and are instead stored in the liver and in fat cells throughout the body. Signs that may indicate an unhappy liver range from: headaches, IBS, poor digestion,

Above: Exercise aids the effective functioning of the internal organs.

bloating, depression and mood changes to the more serious problems of hepatitis and cirrhosis.

The kidneys

These organs basically act as filters to clean the blood. They are responsible for the removal of urea (a toxic waste product from the liver), removal of excess ions (such as sodium) and adjustment of water content in the blood. These waste products are then eliminated in urine, via the bladder. During this filtration process, the kidneys reabsorb useful nutrients and recycle them for further use. It is very important to drink plenty of water at all times to help the kidneys carry out their function efficiently.

The lymphatic system

This system carries toxins, unwanted waste, dead cells and excess fluid to the lymph nodes, where the waste is filtered before being passed into the bloodstream. Poor circulation and a weakened immune system may be signs that the lymphatic system is not functioning efficiently. Higher levels of toxins are believed to slow down your lymphatic system.

The lungs

When we breathe, the lungs deal with air-borne pollutants, such as carbon monoxide from traffic pollution. They allow oxygen to enter the bloodstream and waste products to be removed as carbon dioxide.

Correct breathing is essential if the body's metabolism and organs are to work properly. However many of us do not inhale enough oxygen and so do not expel all the unwanted waste gases. Catarrh, blocked sinuses and a constant runny nose are signs of a poorly functioning respiratory system.

The skin

This is the body's largest organ. Every pore eliminates waste and sweat, and the sebaceous glands help to remove toxins. The skin reflects what is happening inside our bodies. If we are stressed, run down, or have over-indulged, this can show up in a dull, lifeless complexion, or as rashes, spots and blemishes. A healthy diet and drinking plenty of water help to promote clear skin.

Below: Clear skin reflects a healthy digestive system.

How to boost your vital organs

Like a car, the body benefits from a regular service to ensure it runs efficiently and has sufficient energy to fight and eliminate toxins. There are a number of simple, common-sense steps that can help to improve the overall functioning of your vital organs.

The digestive system
• Only eat when you are hungry, and do not overeat or eat large meals late in the evening.
• Take time over meals to eat each mouthful properly and slowly.
• Cut down on refined carbohydrates and foods with a high fat content.
• Do not drink too much with meals as this can dilute your digestive juice.
• Start the day with fruit juices or fruit to boost your digestive system.
• Herbal teas, such as chamomile, peppermint or fennel can be soothing.
• Improve the overall condition of the gut by regularly eating low-fat probiotic yogurt.
• Many herbs and spices are an aid to digestion, so use bay, caraway, cardamom, cinnamon, cumin, dill, fennel, ginger, marjoram, mint, parsley and tarragon in cooking.

The liver
• Drink plenty of water – at least 2 litres/ 4 pints/ 8–9 cups a day.
• Eat plenty of fresh fruit and vegetables, in particular apples, citrus fruits, garlic, beetroot (beets), carrots, broccoli, cabbage, globe artichokes, ginger, green leafy vegetables, and bitter leaves, such as dandelion, as well as whole grains, nuts, seeds and beans.
• Avoid processed, salty, sugary, high-fat and very spicy foods.
• Try to eat mainly organic foods.
• Cut down on alcohol and caffeine.
• Exercise regularly.
• Liver-boosting supplements can help to neutralize free radicals that damage cells. Try an antioxidant supplement containing betacarotene, vitamins C and E and selenium.
• Artichoke extract supplements (containing the compound cynarin) claim to help boost a sluggish liver.

The kidneys
• Drink plenty of water.
• Reduce your intake of animal protein foods, such as meat and dairy products, as these can put a strain on the working of the kidneys.
• Cut down on alcohol.
• Dandelion leaves, tea or supplements can be helpful as a diuretic to treat fluid retention and to help to prevent common kidney problems.

The lymphatic system
• Exercise regularly.
• Stimulate the lymphatic system by exfoliating and skin-brushing.
• Have a massage to encourage the efficiency of the lymphatic system.

Left: Citrus fruits stimulate the digestive system and are powerful cleansers. They are also rich in vitamin C.

BREATHING EXERCISE
Use this exercise to check that you are breathing correctly.

1 Lie with your back on the floor, bend your knees and place your feet on the floor a comfortable distance from your buttocks. Rest your hands flat on your stomach, just below the ribs.

2 Breathe in slowly through your nose, filling your lungs. The lower part of your stomach should rise first. If your chest moves first, you are breathing incorrectly and are not using your diaphragm – this is known as shallow-breathing.

3 Exhale slowly though your nostrils, emptying your lungs – notice your abdomen flattening.

The skin
• Drink plenty of water.
• Eat plenty of fresh fruit and vegetables – preferably raw or juiced. They provide betacarotene (the plant form of vitamin A) and vitamin C, both essential for maintaining healthy skin.
• Choose whole grains, lean protein foods and a moderate intake of polyunsaturated essential fatty acids, found in oily fish, vegetable oils and nuts and seeds.
• Ensure that your diet is not lacking in the mineral zinc. Lean meat, skinless poultry, shellfish and nuts are all good sources and yogurt and skimmed milk also supply useful amounts.
• Restrict convenience foods, high in saturated fats.
• Cut down on chocolate, sweets, highly salted snacks and soft drinks.
• Restrict alcohol intake.
• Boost your circulation by exercising and skin-brushing.
• Get plenty of restful sleep.
• Take regular exercise in the fresh air and breathe deeply.

Foods to avoid

Successful detoxing relies on making both dietary and lifestyle changes in order to allow your body to cleanse itself readily and efficiently. Some of the foods that are off-limits during the detox programme are those known to commonly cause digestive problems and other side effects in susceptible individuals. Others are those widely recognized as best limited or avoided in order to promote a healthy body, thus helping you to retrain your eating habits and make healthy food choices for the long term. These restrictions can be reintroduced in moderation after your detox if you like, unless advised otherwise by a doctor or dietician.

Alcohol

Drinking in moderation can be relaxing and sociable and indeed is reputed to help lower the risk of coronary heart disease if it is kept at a 'sensible' level, but you need to give up drinking alcohol completely while following a detox programme.

Below: Alcoholic drinks in excess place unnecessary strain on the liver.

Above: Tea, coffee, cola drinks and chocolate are all high in caffeine.

Alcohol is basically an extremely toxic compound, and although the liver acts as an efficient detoxifier, breaking down alcohol and converting it into harmless components, this process puts unnecessary strain on the liver, which can become damaged with regular or heavy drinking. Alcohol metabolism also depletes many valuable nutrients, particularly essential fatty acids, vitamins A, C and E, thiamin and zinc, and it acts as a diuretic, causing the kidneys to excrete more fluid along with vital minerals, such as calcium and potassium. This has a dehydration effect on the body.

Alcoholic drinks are also loaded with 'empty' calories (nearly twice as many as sugar) and therefore provide little nutritional value. They may also contain various additives. Sulphites and sulphur-based preservatives are commonly added to wines, beers, ciders and ready-mixed cocktail drinks, which can trigger reactions such as asthma in certain people. Colours and artificial sweeteners may also be added, all increasing the toxic load.

Caffeine

Particularly high levels of caffeine are found in coffee (especially ground coffee), but it is also present in tea, chocolate, colas and some fizzy drinks and in some cold and pain relief tablets. Caffeine is a potent substance that stimulates the brain, heart and central nervous system helping to keep us awake, think clearly and feel brighter. It is also a diuretic, causing loss of calcium and an increased risk of osteoporosis.

While it is the stimulant effect of caffeine that makes drinks containing it popular, caffeine can also act as a laxative and may cause migraines, insomnia, irritability and palpitations, especially if consumed in excessive amounts. More than six cups a day could give rise to high blood pressure and kidney problems. It is also highly addictive, so to avoid withdrawal symptoms you need to cut back on your intake gradually before starting on a detox programme.

Above: Avoid processed meat products such as sausages.

Meat and meat products

Red meat, and meat products especially, are also generally high in saturated fat, although farmers are now breeding animals to be leaner and modern butchery methods have produced leaner cuts. Meat products, such as burgers and sausages, may also contain additives and may be made with low-quality meat, depending on the manufacturer. Moreover, meat creates extra work for the digestive system, so while detoxing it is advisable to take a break from eating it, then to only eat lean cuts of quality meat in moderation after your detox.

Above: Dairy products can be high in saturated fats.

Dairy products and eggs

Cow's milk and dairy products can be difficult to digest for many people and can often cause excessive production of mucous in the sinuses and nasal passages. Yogurt, however, is usually tolerated by most people and provides a good source of calcium. Low-fat probiotic yohurt has a calming effect on the digestive system and can help to maintain a healthy balance of bacteria in the gut. Dairy products, especially butter, cheese and cream, are also the main source of

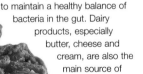

saturated fats in the diet, which healthy eating guidelines advise most people to cut down on.

Eggs may also cause an allergic reaction in susceptible individuals, in which case all eggs and egg products should be excluded from the diet. However, for the majority of people, eggs (ideally organic) can be eaten occasionally and provide an excellent source of protein as well as a range of valuable minerals and vitamins.

Left: Red meat should be avoided during a detox programme, and eaten in moderation at other times.

Above: Cream is very high in saturated fat and should be eaten sparingly. Eat low-fat probiotic yogurt instead.

Wheat products

Coeliacs need to avoid all sources of gluten (the protein found in wheat and also present in barley, rye and oats) permanently. Other individuals may be less seriously intolerant of wheat, but still suffer a mild sensitivity, finding it difficult to digest, and experiencing bloating, constipation and/or diarrhoea. Other grains may be consumed without causing problems.

Common wheat products include bread, flour, pasta, breakfast cereals, couscous and bulgur wheat. Wheat flour is used for making cakes, pies and puddings and is widely used in the manufacture of many processed foods, such as sauce mixes, soups and stuffings. This can make it quite difficult to cut out, although other grains can be substituted. However, it is important to remember that wheat products, especially wholegrain varieties, are nutritious foods and play an important role in a healthy balanced diet. It should therefore not be eliminated from the diet long-term, unless coeliac disease or a true wheat allergy has been diagnosed.

Above: Wheat flour is used in the manufacture of bread, cakes, cookies and pastries.

Salt

A very small amount of salt is a vital constituent of our diet, but we eat far more than our bodies actually need. Most of the salt that we eat is hidden in processed foods; the rest is either added at the table or during cooking. It's now known that our high salt intake has many potentially adverse effects on our health. It is linked with high blood pressure, kidney disease, strokes, stomach cancer and osteoporosis and may play an aggravating role in asthma. It is not a direct cause of asthma, but a high consumption of salt may make the condition worse. High salt intake also increases fluid retention and the tendency to suffer from bloating and swollen ankles and fingers. Simply restricting salt intake to a much lower level can cause fluid loss of up to 2 litres (4 pints) or 2 kg (4½ lb) in body weight. Lemon juice, garlic and herbs and spices can be used instead.

Sugar

This is a very concentrated source of energy that is quickly absorbed into the blood stream, however it has little nutritional value and is high in calories. Avoiding sugary foods and added sugar is therefore a relatively easy way of cutting calories without adversely affecting nutrient intake, especially if you are overweight.

Sugar and refined carbohydrates (as found in chocolate and confectionery, cookies, cakes and pastries) can also be responsible for causing tiredness. This is because they provide a sudden surge of energy, as the enzyme insulin is released and the blood sugar level shoots up, before tumbling again soon afterward – with a resulting feeling of tiredness. The key to maintaining maximum energy is to keep your blood sugar levels constant by eating regular, satisfying meals with a good balance of nutrients and to choose healthy snacks such as fruit, nuts or seeds if peckish in between. Learn to enjoy the natural flavours of food without adding sugar and try not to use artificial sweeteners as an alternative.

Below: Cakes and biscuits contain high amounts of fat and refined sugar.

Above: Fast foods are usually very high in saturated fat, sugar and salt.

Processed foods

Foods that are processed are not intrinsically unhealthy. When you cook, you are processing food at home, but much of the manufactured food that we eat includes large amounts of unhealthy saturated and trans fats, sugars, salt, and chemical additives, which may build up and produce harmful effects in the body. Also the more a food is processed, the more likely it is to have lost some of its nutrient value, particularly vitamins and fibre.

While following a detox programme you should aim to choose fresh, natural food, avoid all additives and to eat as much raw food as possible. Some quality canned foods, not including those packed in brine (high in salt) or syrup (high in sugar), are acceptable as well as being very convenient. So are frozen fruits and vegetables, as they are quickly processed at source and can be more nutritious than fresh food that has been transported over a long distance and displayed for days, or that has been treated after harvesting to lengthen its shelf life.

Fatty and fried foods

Fats provide essential fatty acids, which are vital to the body's metabolism. They also provide a concentrated source of energy, make food more palatable and enable the body to make use of the fat-soluble vitamins, A, D, E and K. However most of us eat too much unhealthy saturated fat, which can raise blood cholesterol levels and increase the risk of heart disease. Calorie-rich, high-fat diets can also lead to obesity.

While following the weekend detox programme, and for long-term healthy eating afterwards, you need to cut down on saturated fat and replace some of it with the healthier unsaturated types. This includes using olive oil (or other vegetable oils high in unsaturates) for cooking, rather than hard fats, and choosing oil-rich fish, such as sardines or mackerel, in preference to red meat.

Below: If you can buy only processed food at work, take in a lunch box instead.

Take-away meals

A take-away (take-out) meal makes an enjoyable treat and occasionally gives you a break from cooking, especially when you are time pressured. However, curries, pizzas, burgers, fried chicken, fish and chips and Chinese dishes are generally loaded with fat and can be difficult to digest. They are also likely to be high in salt, yet lacking in a wide variety of nutrients, especially vitamin C, B group and E, and fibre, and may well contain additives, such as food colours and flavour enhancers that can trigger allergic reactions.

So take a break from these meals while detoxing, although you can still make dishes such as lighter curries and stir-fry dishes, packed with healthy vegetables during the programme, following the recipes in this book. After your detox, take-away meals needn't be banned. Many fast food outlets now offer healthier alternatives, such as grilled chicken salad or chargrilled vegetable kebabs.

Foods to include

You can enjoy a variety of foods while following a weekend detox diet, so you should never feel hungry or find the diet difficult to stick to. It is not designed to be a starvation diet, but includes selected foods that help and encourage the detoxification process while providing a healthy balance of nutrients.

Fruit and vegetables

These are an essential part of a healthy, balanced diet, and all types should be included in abundance on a detox diet. They are highly nutritious, packed with antioxidant vitamins A (as betacarotene), C and E, minerals, fibre and other natural plant compounds, called phytochemicals, which together protect against illness and disease. Antioxidants neutralize free radicals that can damage body cells and increase the risk of cancer.

Be sure to buy fresh-looking produce, ideally that is seasonal and that has been grown locally. Always wash fresh produce before using to remove any chemical residues and choose unwaxed citrus fruits – wash in warm water before use if not unwaxed.

Choose a wide variety of different coloured produce to make sure you are getting a range of nutrients. Eat as snacks, in salads or lightly cooked. Limit potatoes and bananas to no more than three times a week, as they are high in fast-releasing sugars.

Right: Fresh pineapple aids the digestive system.

Super fruits

Apples Studies have revealed that pectin can help protect against the damaging effects of pollution by helping to remove toxins and purify the system. The malic and tartaric acids in apples also benefit the digestion. Apples – if unpeeled – are also a good source of vitamin C, and fibre.

Berries This group includes strawberries, raspberries, blackberries, blackcurrants, cranberries and blueberries. They are rich sources of vitamin C, which helps to fight infection and boost the immune system. Cranberries and blueberries fight harmful bacteria in the kidneys, bladder and urinary tract.

Citrus fruits All are an excellent source of vitamin C. Lemons have a strong cleansing effect and can help relieve gastric problems.

Melons Their high water content is thought to stimulate the kidneys to work more efficiently. Orange-fleshed cantaloupes have the highest vitamin C and betacarotene content.

Left: Fresh melon has a high water content and can stimulate the kidneys.

Papayas Contain an enzyme called papain, which aids the digestion of proteins and benefits the digestive system. It is rich in fibre, betacarotene, vitamin C and phytochemicals with antioxidant properties.

Pineapples Contain the enzyme bromelain, which aids digestion by breaking down proteins and which also has anti-inflammatory properties, which may help relieve arthritis and speed recovery from injuries. It has also been shown to help to relieve sinus congestion and urinary tract infections. Pineapple must be eaten fresh for its healing powers, as bromelain is destroyed in canned pineapple.

Pomegranates Offer good vitamin C and fibre value, and compounds believed to fight disease. New research suggests that the juice may offer many health benefits.

WAKE-UP DRINK

A glass of warm water with some freshly squeezed lemon juice and sliced fresh root ginger added makes the ideal start to the day.

DRIED FRUITS

Excellent snack foods, dried fruits can also be used for making delicious compotes, or as a cooking ingredient in both sweet and savoury dishes to add sweetness and replace added sugar. Dried fruits provide a concentrated source of valuable nutrients and fibre, although they should not be eaten too freely, as due to their natural sugar content, they are quite high in calories, and if eaten between meals, can increase the risk of tooth decay. There is now a fantastic range to choose from, including common favourites like raisins, sultanas (golden raisins), apricots, prunes, figs and dates as well as cranberries, blueberries, cherries and strawberries and mango, apple, papaya, banana and pineapple pieces. Apricots, in particular, are one of the richest fruit sources of iron, a mineral that is frequently lacking in many women's diets. Prunes are well known for their laxative properties, and can help to relieve constipation.

Much dried fruit is treated with sulphur-based preservatives in order to prevent discolouration and to enhance its colour. Apricots and peaches, for example, are a less attractive brown colour if they are left untreated, but if you want to avoid additives, particularly during a detox, choose unsulphured fruit. It is also important to note that sulphured foods can trigger asthma attacks in susceptible people. Potassium-based preservatives are also sometimes added to ready-to-eat dried fruit (which is partially hydrated to be softer than normal dried fruit) to prevent fungal and bacterial spoilage. The best policy is to always check the ingredients' label, as all additives must be listed.

Right: Carrots are good for the immune system and help to maintain healthy skin and eyes.

Carrots Rich in the antioxidant betacarotene (as evident in their bright orange colour) which is good for the immune system as well as for skin and eye health. Unlike the vitamin and mineral content of many vegetables, the betacarotene is better absorbed if the carrots are cooked.

Celery A good, low-calorie diuretic that helps the kidneys to function efficiently and so hastens the excretion of waste. It may also help to lower cholesterol levels and blood pressure. Use in soups, salads and stir-fries.

Below: Broccoli is packed with goodness and is a powerful antioxidant.

Super vegetables

Beetroot (beet) A powerful blood cleanser and tonic and valued for its value to the digestive system and the liver particularly. It is rich in potassium and provides plenty of folate and iron, essential for the formation of red blood cells and helping to prevent anaemia. It has a reputation for stimulating the immune system and may also help to combat cancer, although this has yet to be proved scientifically. Choose fresh raw or cooked beetroot, but not the type packed in vinegar, because as well as being acidic and therefore an irritant to a sensitive gut, pickling reduces the level of nutrients.

Broccoli A cruciferous vegetable – along with cauliflower, kale cabbage, spring greens (collards), turnips, Brussels sprouts, kale and radishes – rich in carotenoids (phytochemicals), which are powerful antioxidants thought to suppress the formation of free radicals and protect against certain cancers. Broccoli also provides iron and is an excellent source of folate, vitamin C and potassium.

Left: Beetroot contains many beneficial properties that can cleanse the blood and aid the digestive system.

Leabharlanna Poibli Chathair Bhaile Átha Cliath
Dublin City Public Libraries

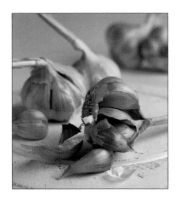

Above: Garlic is one of the most potent natural healers.

Garlic Highly valued for its anti-viral and anti-bacterial properties and many therapeutic benefits. It is a natural decongestant, helps to fight infections and eliminate toxins and may lower cholesterol levels, reduce blood pressure and help to prevent cancer.

Ginger Knobbly-looking, fresh root ginger is valued as an aid to digestion as well as being good for combating colds, stimulating the appetite, improving circulation and helping to alleviate nausea. It's also reputed to help relieve rheumatic pains.

Globe artichokes A substance called cynarin, found in the base of the vegetable leaves, may help liver function and control cholesterol levels.

Onions Like garlic, well known as a cure-all, with an impressive reputation for helping with all kinds of ailments. They have powerful antibiotic properties and are great natural decongestants.

Pumpkin and other squash Supplies a good source of the antioxidants beta-carotene and vitamin E. The flesh is easily digested, and they rarely cause allergies, which makes them an excellent detox food.

FRESH GINGER TEA

Infuse 1 tbsp peeled and grated fresh root ginger in boiling water for 5 minutes. Strain before drinking.

Spinach This and all salad leaves provide antioxidants, vital for healthy immune function. The darker the leaves, the higher their nutrient value.

Tomatoes A rich source of the antioxidant lycopene. Cooking and processing releases this lycopene, so there is even more in tomato products such as tomato purée (paste), passata (bottled strained tomatoes) and canned tomatoes. All can be included on the detox diet, although tomatoes can aggravate eczema and trigger migraine in some people.

Watercress Rich in antioxidant vitamins and minerals and reputed to help speed up the body's detoxification process and purify the blood. It is a natural antibiotic, can help to promote a clear skin and is reputed to help relieve

---

SEA VEGETABLES

Seaweeds, or sea vegetables as they are now known, are highly nutritious. They absorb and concentrate nutrients present in the sea and provide a rich supply of minerals, such as calcium, iodine and iron, and vitamins, including vitamin B12, which is not found in land vegetables. In Japan, where sea vegetables are widely produced in the coastal waters, they are highly valued for the protection they provide against toxic substances, for their intestinal-cleansing qualities, and for helping to combat acidity in the body, which is caused by over-consumption of coffee and alcohol.

Much of the seaweed sold is in a cleaned, dried and packaged form, under its Japanese species name, such as nori, wakame or kombu, but varieties are also harvested in coastal areas around Europe, including Welsh laverbread and Irish carragheen. Dried types are convenient for keeping in the store cupboard (pantry), and

then can be soaked before using (including the soaking water). Nori is most commonly used for making sushi, but sea vegetables generally can be added to soups, stews and salads. They go well with rice and potato dishes and have a special affinity with fish.

Kelp tablets are a convenient way of including some seaweed in the diet. They can be readily bought from most health food stores.

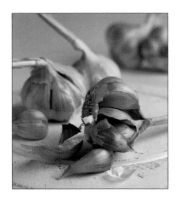

Above: Watercress is a natural antibiotic and can relieve a number of complaints.

stomach upsets, respiratory problems and urinary tract complaints. Eat in generous portions.

SPROUTS

All sprouts can be eaten fresh and raw in salads and provide a rich source of valuable vitamins and minerals, as well as protein. Bean sprouts, cress and sometimes alfalfa, can be bought quite readily, but it is also quick and easy to grow your own. The best known and easiest to sprout are mung and aduki beans, chick peas, whole lentils, mustard and cress (fine curled cress), fenugreek and alfalfa seeds. Try to buy seeds that have not been treated with pesticides; they are often available in health stores.

Above: A wide range of nutritious grains provide variety in the diet.

Dried beans, peas and lentils

These are a great source of low-fat, vegetable protein as well as B vitamins and a wide range of minerals, including iron and magnesium. They also have a high fibre value, which helps to prevent and relieve constipation and lower blood cholesterol, reducing the risk of heart disease and stroke. There is a wide variety of different beans, peas and lentils to choose from, and they can all be included on a detox diet.

Dried beans and peas (but not lentils) require soaking overnight. Soak in cold water, then drain, rinse and cook in fresh, unsalted water. Bring to the boil, then boil rapidly for 10 minutes to destroy any toxins, then simmer gently for 1–1½ hours, or as advised on the packet instructions. If using canned varieties, choose those canned in water or with reduced salt and rinse thoroughly before using. They are very versatile and satisfying to eat and present all kinds of delicious detoxing recipe possibilities, including soups, salads, dips and casseroles. They can be mostly interchanged in recipes.

Left: Do not add salt to the water when cooking dried beans, peas and lentils as this prevents them from softening.

Whole grains

These provide slow-releasing carbohydrate for sustained energy and should be eaten regularly. During a detox, it is advised that wheat and wheat products are avoided, but there are many other cereal grains that can be substituted. These can include rye, barley and oats (unless a gluten intolerance is diagnosed), millet, corn, buckwheat or quinoa and rice.

Whole grains make the best choice as they have a higher fibre value than refined types, as well as providing a good supply of B and E vitamins, minerals and small amounts of essential oils. Brown rice is particularly efficient at cleansing the digestive system. It is also anti-allergenic and helps to stabilize blood sugar levels. Quinoa is another easily digested cleansing grain that is a good source of protein, B vitamins, minerals and fibre. It has a nutty flavour and can be steamed or boiled and eaten like rice. Corn, millet or buckwheat pastas, or rice noodles can all be substituted for wheat pasta.

Mycoprotein (Quorn)

Quorn is made from mycoprotein, a plant that is related to mushrooms and truffles. It makes a versatile and nourishing alternative to meat that is easily digested, although it is best to choose the mince, pieces or fillets as an ingredient, rather than ready-prepared recipe dishes, while following a detox diet. Quorn is high in quality protein, low in fat and contains no cholesterol, yet provides a good source of fibre, which helps to fill you up. It is quick and easy to use and versatile for a range of dishes from salads to stir-fries. Note that Quorn contains egg albumen, so it is not suitable for people with a true egg allergy.

Tofu

Made from soya bean curd, tofu provides a healthy and versatile rich source of dairy-free, vegetable protein. It contains all eight essential amino acids making it an excellent alternative to meat. It is also low in saturated fat and sodium, cholesterol-free and provides useful amounts of calcium, iron and B-group vitamins. It is a completely natural product and contains no artificial additives. Furthermore, soya products are rich in phytoestrogens, which can help to lower blood cholesterol and relieve menopausal symptoms and may help to prevent breast and prostate cancers and osteoporosis.

Tofu is sold in a variety of forms, the most common of which are chilled firm tofu, and silken tofu, which has a silky, smooth

Above: Nutritious tofu is a wonderfully versatile ingredient.

texture like yogurt or custard. Firm tofu can be sliced or cut into cubes and used for dishes such as salads, kebabs and stir-fries, or blended for soups, dips, dressings, spreads and desserts.

Silken tofu is best suited for making desserts, soups, dressings and smoothies. Tofu has an ability to absorb and enhance whatever flavour or other ingredients it's mixed with. Other forms of tofu are available, including smoked, marinated and deep-fried tofu, but these are best avoided during a detox.

Left: Mycoprotein has a meat-like texture, yet in contrast to animal protein, it contains dietary fibre in addition to high protein levels.

IDEAS FOR USING TOFU

- Mash the tofu and make it into burgers with onion, herbs, spices and garlic.
- Use as a salad dressing: blend with chopped fresh coriander (cilantro) leaves and lemon juice.
- Thread cubes on to skewers with mushrooms, tomatoes and (bell) peppers; marinate in soy sauce and mustard before grilling.
- Whip with fresh herbs and Tabasco sauce as a dip for carrot sticks and other crudités.

- Blend with fresh fruit, such as strawberries or raspberries, to make a fruit fool.
- Stir-fry with Chinese mushrooms, bamboo shoots, pak choi (bok choy) and cashew nuts.
- Poach in a clear broth with seafood and vegetable strips for a simple, light meal.

Above: A light oil and vinegar dressing perks up a simple leafy salad without adding masses of fat and calories.

Oils and vinegars

Vegetable oils provide essential fatty aids (omega-6 and omega-3) and are also a good source of vitamin E. They are made from nuts, seeds, beans, peas and lentils, the most common being sunflower, safflower, rapeseed, corn, olive and soya bean, and consist of varying ratios of monounsaturated and polyunsaturated fatty acids. Any of these can be used in small quantities while following a detox diet. Speciality oils, including walnut, sesame and hazelnut oils can also be lightly sprinkled over salads and stir-fries.

Cold-pressed oils, where the oil has been pressed out rather than extracted by heat, retain more vitamin E, but these oils especially must not be kept for long periods, as they do not keep well, lose their vitamin E when exposed to sunlight and are prone to rancidity. Store oils in a cool dark place and buy in small quantities. Also, do not reuse cooking oils because constant reheating sets off a chemical reaction that can create free radicals.

Cider vinegar makes the best choice of vinegar during a detox. It is made from fermented apple juice and is reputed to have many therapeutic properties including helping to ease arthritic pains and stimulating the liver to produce more bile. It may also help the digestion, regulate metabolism, cure gastro-intestinal infections and diarrhoea, and help to relieve chronic fatigue.

Vital water

Drink at least 2 litres/4 pints/8–9 cups of water each day to help flush out toxins and waste products and to avoid fluid retention. Drinking sufficient water also helps to prevent urinary infections, constipation, headaches and bloating and helps to keep your skin clear. It can be drunk as herbal teas or with freshly squeezed fruit or vegetable juice. Drink plenty of fluids throughout the day, but do not drink to excess. There is no benefit in doing so, and it will just be an inconvenience if you need to visit the toilet frequently.

Herbal teas

Also called tisanes or infusions, herbal and fruit teas provide a refreshing, alternative hot drink to coffee, regular black tea and hot chocolate or cocoa, while following a detox diet. These drinks are naturally caffeine-free as well as sugar-free and contain virtually no calories. They are usually enjoyed without milk or added sugar, and are equally good drunk chilled. The myriad of flavours available is a bonus too, ensuring that the taste buds will never be bored, and you can choose various flavours to suit different moods and times of the day, depending on whether you need to perk up or calm down. Some teas are also reputed to help ease common complaints such as a queasy stomach or an aching head.

HEALTH BENEFITS OF HERBAL TEAS

• Chamomile tea is well known for helping to promote a good night's sleep. You could also try adding a chamomile tea bag to your bath to help yourself relax.
• Lemon verbena, peppermint and fennel are all valued for their calming digestive properties, making them ideal as an after-meal soother.
• Mixed fruit, rosehip, cinnamon, ginger and orange blossom offer awakening, revitalizing properties for when you need a pick-me-up.
• Rooibosch (Redbush) tea, made from a South African herb, contains highly beneficial flavonoids and trace minerals and has been scientifically proved to possess both anti-inflammatory and anti-spasmodic properties, offering relief to many allergy sufferers. It may help to relieve both digestive and skin complaints.
• Parsley tea is a great general aid for the kidneys. Infuse fresh parsley in boiling water for 5 minutes.

Below: Herbal teas make a perfect detox drink choice.

Detox supplements

If following a healthy balanced diet, supplements should not be necessary for most people. However, there are a number of specific supplements, recommended by natural practitioners, that are claimed to help with the detoxification process and that may also be beneficial in helping to relieve certain ailments and conditions.

Aloe vera

Taken as a drink, the juice of this succulent plant is believed to help cleanse and detoxify, boost the immune system and promote greater energy. It also is reputed to be beneficial in helping to relieve a wide range of conditions, including many digestive disorders, allergies, rheumatism and arthritis.

Artichoke extract

Globe artichoke is a member of the milk thistle family. Cynarin, a compound extracted from the artichoke leaves, is thought to help improve liver function, control cholesterol levels and help the gut to break down fats. It is recommended for digestive disorders, helping to relieve indigestion, a bloated feeling and IBS symptoms.

Below: Globe artichokes contain compounds that assist liver function.

Right: Kelp is a form of edible seaweed. It is rich in iodine and can be taken in tablet form, or consumed fresh or dried in soups, salads and dips.

Chlorella and spirulina

These freshwater algae supplements contain a high concentration of chlorophyll and are an excellent source of many essential nutrients, which act as powerful antioxidants. They are claimed to be good blood tonics and cleansers, helping to promote the digestive system by acting as an 'intestinal broom' and removing toxins, boosting the immune system and promoting energy.

Co-enzyme Q10

The full name for this vitamin-like substance is ubiquinol, and it plays an important role in the body's metabolic processes, particularly in the release of energy from food. It is also an excellent antioxidant. It can be made in the body (unlike vitamins that need to be digested) and is found in some foods, but it may not always be synthesized in sufficient quantity, and also levels tend to decline with age. It has been shown to have a stimulating effect on the immune system and may help increase resistance to viral infections, reduce the toxicity of immune-suppressive drugs, alleviate allergic symptoms, help prevent gum disease and help protect against arthritis and other degenerative diseases. It may also help to maintain healthy blood pressure and strengthen the heart and may be prescribed for people with high cholesterol or who are obese or lacking in energy.

Dandelion

Recommended for helping to relieve poor digestion and water retention, and it may also help to cleanse the blood and treat skin disorders, such as eczema. Bitter compounds in the leaves and root act as a general stimulant to the digestive system, especially the urinary organs. It is well known as a traditional diuretic, but with the benefit of not causing potassium depletion, since the dandelion's own potassium content replaces that which may be lost in the urine. Dandelion can also help to increase bile production in the gall bladder and bile flow from the liver, which helps to improve fat (including cholesterol) metabolism. It is a great tonic for sluggish liver function, resulting from poor diet and excess alcohol consumption. You can take dandelion root capsules or add young leaves, gathered from the countryside, to salads. The leaves contain betacarotene and calcium, as well as potassium and more iron than spinach.

Ginkgo biloba

This is excellent for the circulation and is thought to be good for boosting memory as it aids the blood flow to the brain.

Kelp

This form of marine algae is best known for its high iodine content, a mineral that is needed for the thyroid gland to function normally. Kelp tablets (and fresh and dried seaweeds) have long been used in traditional medicine to help treat colds, constipation, arthritis and rheumatism.

Liquorice
This root has a mild anti-inflammatory effect and can help relieve the symptoms of most allergies. However, it should not be used alongside steroid medication or by anyone who suffers from high blood pressure, as it can cause the retention of sodium and the depletion of potassium. Liquorice is available as a root from most health food stores. Grind the root with a mortar and pestle or buy pure powdered root.

Milk thistle
This herb is often recommended to counter-balance the effects of a modern lifestyle, stress, pollution and over-consumption of rich 'junk' foods. It is a powerful liver detoxifier and antioxidant, helping to protect and regenerate liver cells. As well as helping the liver to work more efficiently, this herb increases the secretion and flow of bile from the gall bladder, increasing the body's ability to digest heavy fatty foods. Health conditions where milk thistle is useful include liver problems, such as hepatitis and cirrhosis, over-burden from drugs and hormones, skin conditions such as psoriasis and gall bladder problems.

Probiotics
These are live, beneficial bacteria essential for the healthy functioning of the gut. In a healthy body they are present naturally, but frequently the stores are depleted by the use of antibiotics, illness or by eating a diet high in refined sugars. To help restore a good balance, you should eat live probiotic yogurt regularly or you can take tablet supplements.

Psyllium husks
These are the crushed seeds of the herb plant, plantain, and as a supplement, should be taken with plenty of water. They are rich in soluble fibre, which is good for cleansing the colon, speeding up the passage of waste materials and acting as a gentle laxative. They are also effective in helping to lower blood cholesterol levels and reducing the risk of heart disease.

Rosehip
The reddish-orange fruit of the wild rose (dog rose) has extremely high levels of vitamin C. Fresh hedgerow rosehips can be stewed then strained, to use in drinks. Alternatively, you can buy rosehip tea or tablets. Avoid rosehip syrup as it is very high in sugar.

Wheatgrass
This is a widely used, popular supplement that is available in tablet form, but that can also be bought fresh, from health food stores or home-grown, to use for juicing. It is another potent detoxifier and cleanser, due to its high

Left: Rosehips appear around late summer/early autumn and can be found growing wild in many hedgerows. Use them to make drinks high in vitamin C.

chlorophyll and nutrient content, providing a rich source of B vitamins, plus vitamins A, C and E, as well as many minerals. It is reputed to have many healing properties. Despite being sprouted from grain plants and called wheatgrass, it is gluten-free.

Left: Wheatgrass, rich in chlorophyll (known as nature's healer) is a powerful detoxifier and cleanser.

GUIDELINES
• Always read the label and follow the recommended dosage and guidelines, especially if you are pregnant or have a medical condition. Supplements can be dangerous if the dose is exceeded or the guidlines not adhered to.
• Buy supplements that are as natural as possible, ideally without artificial colourings or flavourings, gelatin coatings or fillers.
• Generally supplements are best absorbed if eaten with food or just after a meal, but follow the instructions on the pack.
• If in doubt about taking any supplement, take advice from a qualified naturopath, a pharmacist or your family doctor, especially if taking medication for a condition. Supplements can interfere with other drugs and supplements, so always seek medical advice.
• Store all supplements in a cool, dry place and safely out of the reach of children.
• Follow the 'use by' date.

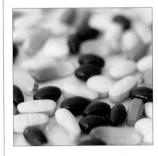

A weekend detox

A weekend detox is an excellent introduction to detoxing and provides an opportunity to take some time out from a hectic lifestyle to concentrate just on your own well-being. Use this programme as a short refresher to relax and give your health a boost. This weekend detox is a strict regime based on fruit and vegetable dishes and juices, so it should only be followed for two days and no longer.

A weekend detox programme is designed to give your digestive system a rest, allowing it to concentrate on eliminating stored toxins. It is based on three light meals a day – breakfast, lunch and dinner, but you can also have fruit and raw vegetable snacks during the day. It is essential to drink plenty of water, as well as vitamin-rich juices and herbal teas. Raw fruit and vegetables have a powerful cleansing effect on the body and also supply plenty of vitamins, minerals and fibre.

Above: Give your body a boost before you start the weekend detox by enjoying a delicious nutrient-packed drink, such as Banana and Mango Smoothie.

Below: Cut down on chocolate before starting a detox programme.

Timing
Choose a weekend when you are free to completely rest and relax. You will gain the greatest benefit from your detox if you can fully devote yourself to the regime without distractions and not feel under pressure from anyone.

Preparation
• Prepare for your detox by gradually cutting down on all the 'Foods to avoid' up to one week before. This will help your body to adjust more easily to the restricted eating plan and also help to prevent withdrawal symptoms from reducing or cutting out addictive food and drinks, like chocolate and coffee.
• Clean and tidy the bathroom giving yourself a relaxing and calming environment where you can retreat for some time to pamper yourself undisturbed.

• Remove from your kitchen cupboard any items of food that should be avoided during a detox.
• Let friends and family know about your detox plans so they can help out with household jobs or perhaps looking after children. They can also provide you with motivation and support.

Above: Reduce your intake of caffeine gradually before a detox to avoid withdrawal symptoms.

Friday

Make sure that your diary is free and that you have no urgent work or household chores that need doing or that will prevent you from relaxing completely for the whole weekend. Avoid subjecting yourself to stressful situations that may cause anxiety.

Shop for all the food that you will need over the course of the weekend and cook a healthy light meal for the Friday evening that will be easy to digest. A vegetable soup or a stir-fry would be ideal.

Dinner Here are some suitable recipe ideas – but you can choose something else, if you prefer, from the selection of recipes in this book.

- Spicy Pumpkin Soup
- Mixed Bean Salad
- Mushroom Rice with Cashew Nuts
- Spring Vegetable Stir-fry
- Harvest Vegetable and Lentil Casserole
- Barley Risotto with Roasted Squash and Leeks
- Fresh Fruit with Mango Coulis

Below: An exotic fruit salad is delicious and packed with vitamin power.

Above: A warm bath is relaxing and helps to improve circulation.

TOP TIPS

Do not drink any alcohol and try to avoid smoking to ensure that you have a good night's sleep. Soak in a relaxing aromatherapy bath before retiring, then go to bed early with a good book or perhaps listen to a story on the radio.

Below: Barley Risotto makes a tasty, light and nutritious main meal.

Saturday

Morning Rise and shine with a cup of warm water flavoured with the juice of half a lemon. This will give a kick-start to the liver. Do some simple stretching exercise to stimulate the lymphatic system. Give yourself a dry skin brush to stimulate your circulation, then take a shower or warm bath.

Breakfast Fragrant Fruit Salad, or any other alternative fruit salad or smoothie.

Morning Exercise Take a brisk walk, go cycling or do any other form of exercise you enjoy. Sip water at regular intervals. When you have finished, eat some fresh or dried fruit or raw vegetable crudités, and drink a herbal tea. You could also have some unsalted nuts or seeds, if you are feeling hungry.

Morning Activity Choose from the list of ideas on page 34.

Lunch Choose a chilled tomato or vegetable juice or a juice from the recipe section, followed by a large salad with a light dressing. If it is a cold day, choose a vegetable soup instead. Good choices might include:
• Carrot and Celery Juice
• Red Pepper and Sprout Salad with Cashew Cream Dressing
• Borlotti Bean and Vegetable Soup

Above: Borlotti Bean and Vegetable Soup is served ladled over spinach.

Afternoon Relax with a book or a complementary therapy such as a massage or reflexology treatment. Follow with some free time to put your feet up to enjoy a good book, watch a film or listen to relaxing music. Drink a herbal tea or a refreshing juice. Good choices might include:
• Blueberry Tonic
• Cinnamon and Squash Smoothie

Dinner Between 6 and 8pm have your evening meal. This should be a lightly cooked vegetable dish served with wholegrain rice so that it is healthy yet satisfying. Follow this with a fresh fruit salad, topped with low-fat probiotic yogurt. Good recipe choices might include:
• Roasted Vegetables with Salsa Verde
• Stir-fried Rice and Vegetables
• Spanish-style Vegetables with Thyme

Left: Cinnamon and Squash Smoothie is made with vitamin-rich butternut squash and is as filling as it is delicious.

Evening
Practise a relaxation technique such as meditation or visualization. Pamper yourself with a manicure or pedicure. Have an Epsom salts bath, then relax with a book or calming music and a drink of chamomile or peppermint tea.

Below: Meditation is a great way to relax your mind.

Above: Spanish-style Vegetables with Thyme is a taste sensation.

Sunday

Take it easy as you may feel tired, cold or nauseous today. This is because your body could be experiencing a "cleansing crisis", which is when toxins previously stored in fat cells are released into the system in order to be flushed away. These side effects indicate that your body is beginning to eliminate toxins.

Repeat the same routine as followed on Saturday, but choose different fruit and vegetable juices, different soups, salads or hot vegetable dishes for meal times and other exercises, therapies and activities. Choose things that you enjoy to make the most of your weekend and to reap the greatest benefits both physically and mentally. **Note**: Do not have an Epsom salts bath today, but soak in a relaxing aromatherapy bath before bedtime.

The day after detoxing

It is important to ease your body out of a detox gradually. So do not rush into anything too energetic or stressful or return to an unhealthy pattern of eating and drinking. Continue to eat a healthy, balanced diet that is low in saturated fats and salt, and that incorporates a wide range of fresh, seasonal foods. Try to maintain the habit of making time to exercise and relax on a daily basis.

Right: Reading can help to draw the mind away from everyday cares.

DETOX WEEKEND ACTIVITY IDEAS

Use this time to do some of the activities you have been meaning to do for ages, but have not had time to get around to. Here are some simple activity ideas:

• De-clutter drawers and cupboards. You will feel so much more clear-headed if your home is well organized and free of unnecessary junk.
• Clear out your wardrobe, removing all items that do not fit, do not suit or that look drab or dated.
• Make phone calls to friends or relations that you have not spoken to for a while.
• Go through old magazines and make a recipe file of delicious-looking healthy recipes to add to the ones in this book.
• Arrange old photographs into albums and enjoy a trip down memory lane.

• Start to learn a new language. Choose whichever form of media you prefer. You could also investigate joining a class in your area.
• Try solving absorbing word or number puzzles.
• Take up a new hobby such as watercolour painting or knitting.
• Start a birthday book, a new address book or diary.
• Defrost the freezer and throw out old stock or any highly processed foods.
• Plant up containers and window boxes with fresh herbs or do some work in the garden.
• Make a list of ways you would like to improve your life and brainstorm how you might put these into action.
• Watch a good film that you have always wanted to see.

juices, smoothies and breakfast ideas

Start each day with a nourishing and sustaining breakfast.
Many traditional breakfast foods such as wheat cereals and toast
will not be an option while following a detox diet, but there are
plenty of other delicious alternatives. Fruit and vegetables
are rich in vitamins and high in fibre and have a powerful
effect on the body, stimulating the digestive system.
Enjoy them as juices, smoothies and fruit salads.

Cinnamon and squash smoothie

Lightly cooked butternut squash makes a delicious, vitamin-packed smoothie. It has a wonderfully rich, rounded flavour that is lifted perfectly by the addition of tart citrus juice and warm, spicy cinnamon. Imagine pumpkin pie as a gorgeous smooth drink and you're halfway to experiencing the flavours of this lusciously sweet and tantalizing treat.

1 Halve the squash, scoop out and discard the seeds and cut the flesh into chunks. Cut away the skin and discard. Steam or boil the squash for 10–15 minutes until just tender. Drain well and leave to stand until cool.

2 Put the cooled squash in a blender or food processor and add the ground cinnamon. Squeeze the lemons and grapefruit and pour the juice over the squash. Add the honey, if using.

3 Process the ingredients until they are very smooth. If necessary, pause to scrape down the side of the food processor or blender.

4 Put a few ice cubes in two or three short glasses and pour over the smoothie. Serve immediately.

Serves 2–3

1 small butternut squash,
    about 600g/1lb 6oz
2.5ml/½ tsp ground cinnamon
3 large lemons
1 grapefruit
clear honey, to taste
ice cubes

Cook's tip
Squash are not only delicious, but they also contain high levels of magnesium and potassium and are low in calories. If you can only buy a large squash, cook it all and add the leftovers to a stew or soup.

Energy 43Kcal/180kJ; Protein 1.6g; Carbohydrate 8.5g, of which sugars 7.5g; Fat 0.4g, of which saturates 0.2g; Cholesterol 0mg; Calcium 65mg; Fibre 2g; Sodium 4mg.

Carrot and celery juice

This juice is so packed with goodness, you can almost feel it cleansing and detoxing your body. As well as valuable vitamins, the carrots and grapes provide plenty of natural sweetness, which blends perfectly with the mild pepperiness of the celery and fresh scent of parsley. Drink this juice on a regular basis to give your system a thorough clean-out.

Serves 1–2

1 celery stick
300g/11oz carrots
150g/5oz green grapes
several large sprigs of parsley
celery or carrot sticks, to serve

1 Using a sharp knife, roughly chop the celery and carrots. Push half of the celery, carrots and grapes through a juicer, then add the parsley sprigs. Add the remaining celery, carrots and grapes in the same way and juice until thoroughly combined.

2 Pour into one or two glasses and serve with celery or carrot stick stirrers.

Health benefits

When juicing herbs, do not remove their individual stalks because it is the stalks that contain much of the goodness and flavour – and they go through the juicing machine very easily. Parsley contains useful amounts of vitamin C and iron and also works as a natural cleanser and breath freshener.

Energy 77Kcal/322kJ; Protein 1.2g; Carbohydrate 17.9g, of which sugars 17.1g; Fat 0.6g, of which saturates 0.2g; Cholesterol 0mg; Calcium 53mg; Fibre 3.8g; Sodium 50mg.

Blueberry tonic

Blueberries are not only an excellent source of antioxidant vitamins, they are also rich in antibacterial compounds that can help to prevent gastric and urinary infections. Mixed with dark red fruits, such as blackberries and grapes, they make a highly nutritious and extremely delicious blend that can be enjoyed throughout the day.

Serves 1

90g/3½oz/scant 1 cup blackcurrants
  or blackberries
150g/5oz red grapes
130g/4½oz/generous 1 cup blueberries
ice cubes

1 Remove the blackcurrants, if using, and grapes from their stalks.

2 Push all the fruits through a juicer, saving a few for decoration.

3 Place the ice cubes in a medium glass and pour over the juice. Decorate with the remaining fruit and serve the juice immediately.

Cook's tip
This is a very tangy wake-up drink that can be diluted with chilled mineral water, if you like. Sweeten with a little honey if you find the taste a bit too sharp.

Energy 149Kcal/639kJ; Protein 1.6g; Carbohydrate 37.7g, of which sugars 37.7g; Fat 0.2g, of which saturates 0g; Cholesterol 0mg; Calcium 90mg; Fibre 4.2g; Sodium 12mg.

Orange and raspberry smoothie

This exquisite blend combines the sharp-sweet taste of raspberries and the refreshing fruitiness of oranges with smooth yogurt. It tastes like creamy fruit heaven in a glass. Even better, it takes just minutes to prepare, making it perfect as a quick breakfast juice for boosting the immune system. It may also be enjoyed as a refreshing drink at any other time of day.

Serves 2

250g/9oz/1⅓ cups raspberries, washed and chilled
200ml/7fl oz/scant 1 cup low-fat probiotic yogurt, chilled
300ml/½ pint/1¼ cups freshly squeezed orange juice, chilled

1 Place the raspberries and yogurt in a blender or food processor and process for about 1 minute until the mixture is smooth and creamy.

2 Add the orange juice to the raspberry and yogurt mixture and process for another 30 seconds. Pour into tall glasses and serve immediately.

Cook's tip
For a super-chilled version, use frozen raspberries instead of fresh. You may need to blend the raspberries and yogurt for a little longer to get a smooth result.

Energy 142Kcal/602kJ; Protein 7.6g; Carbohydrate 26.5g, of which sugars 26.5g; Fat 1.5g, of which saturates 0.7g; Cholesterol 1mg; Calcium 237mg; Fibre 3.3g; Sodium 102mg.

Banana and mango smoothie

Easy to prepare and even easier to drink, this energy-packed smoothie makes a great start to the day. Bananas provide the perfect fuel in the form of slow-release carbohydrate that will keep you going all morning, while vitamin C-rich orange juice and sweet, scented mango will set your tastebuds tingling first thing.

Serves 2

1 mango
1 large banana
1 large orange
15ml/1 tbsp sesame seeds

Health benefits
Sesame seeds not only taste delicious, but they also provide a good source of vitamin E, as well as some calcium. For extra fibre value, add 25ml/1½ tbsp medium oatmeal to the smoothie.

1 Using a small, sharp knife, skin the mango, then slice the flesh off the stone (pit). Peel the banana and break it into short lengths, then place it in a blender or food processor with the mango flesh.

2 Squeeze the juice from the orange and add to the blender or food processor along with the sesame seeds. Whizz until the mixture is smooth and creamy, then pour into glasses and serve.

Energy 148Kcal/625kJ; Protein 3.1g; Carbohydrate 25g, of which sugars 23.9g; Fat 4.7g, of which saturates 0.8g; Cholesterol 0mg; Calcium 90mg; Fibre 4g; Sodium 7mg.

Fragrant fruit salad

Fruit salads are wonderfully versatile and can include any variety of fresh fruit to suit the season. They can be as simple as you like or fabulously exciting, made with exotic foreign fruits, as typified in this recipe, which includes pineapple, papaya, pomegranate, mango and passion fruit. Fruit salads are best eaten shortly after making, to preserve their full vitamin value.

Serves 4

1 small pineapple
120ml/4 fl oz/½ cup fresh, chilled
   apple juice
juice of 1 lime
1 papaya
1 mango
2 pomegranates
2 passion fruits or kiwi fruit
fine strips of lime peel, to decorate

1 Using a sharp knife, cut the plume and stalk ends from the pineapple.

2 Peel and cut the flesh into bitesize pieces, discarding the core. Put into a serving bowl.

3 Pour over the apple juice and lime juice and stir the mixture together to combine thoroughly.

4 Halve the papaya and scoop out the seeds using a spoon. Cut away the skin with a sharp knife, then cut the flesh into chunks.

5 Cut the mango lengthways into three pieces, along each side of the stone (pit). Peel the skin off the flesh. Cut into chunks and add to the bowl.

6 Halve the pomegranates and scoop out the seeds. Add to the bowl.

7 Halve the passion fruits and scoop out the flesh using a teaspoon or peel and chop the kiwi fruit. Add to the bowl and serve, decorated with lime peel.

Health benefits
Pomegranate is rich in antioxidants and offers good vitamin C and fibre content, plus lots of visual appeal.

Energy 104Kcal/446kJ; Protein 1.3g; Carbohydrate 25.5g, of which sugars 25.4g; Fat 0.4g, of which saturates 0.1g; Cholesterol 0mg; Calcium 46mg; Fibre 4.2g; Sodium 13mg.

simply sensational soups

Soups are full of vegetable goodness and provide tempting and satisfying lunch or supper dishes all year round, whatever the weather. Tuck into classic favourites such as Carrot and Orange Soup or Spicy Pumpkin Soup, or treat your tastebuds to Russian Borscht with Kvas or Butter Bean, Tomato and Pesto Soup.

  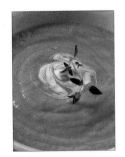

Carrot and orange soup

This bright and summery soup with a vibrantly fresh citrus flavour is packed with antioxidant vitamins. Use a good, home-made vegetable stock made with fresh ingredients and no artificial flavourings or excess salt. Here the soup is served warm, but you could chill it in the refrigerator for a few hours and serve it cold on a hot summer's day.

Serves 4

30ml/2 tbsp olive oil
3 leeks, sliced
450g/1lb carrots, sliced
1.2 litres/2 pints/5 cups vegetable stock
rind and juice of 2 oranges
2.5ml/½ tsp freshly grated nutmeg
150ml/¼ pint/⅔ cup low-fat probiotic yogurt
5ml/1 tsp cornflour (cornstarch)
ground black pepper
fresh sprigs of coriander (cilantro),
    to garnish

1 Heat the oil in a large pan. Add the leeks and carrots and stir well, coating the vegetables with the oil. Cover and cook for about 10 minutes, until the vegetables are beginning to soften but not colour.

2 Pour in the stock and the orange rind and juice. Add the nutmeg and season to taste with ground black pepper. Bring to the boil, lower the heat, cover and simmer for about 40 minutes, or until the vegetables are tender.

3 Leave to cool slightly, then purée the soup in a food processor or blender until smooth.

4 Return the soup to the pan. Blend 30ml/2 tbsp of the yogurt with the cornflour, then stir into the soup. Taste and adjust the seasoning, if necessary. Reheat gently.

5 Ladle the soup into warm individual bowls and put a swirl of yogurt in the centre of each. Sprinkle with coriander and serve immediately.

Energy 135Kcal/564kJ; Protein 3.9g; Carbohydrate 16.1g, of which sugars 15g; Fat 6.6g, of which saturates 1.2g; Cholesterol 1mg; Calcium 120mg; Fibre 4.4g; Sodium 63mg.

Pea soup with garlic

This delicious, simple soup has a wonderfully sweet taste and smooth texture, and is really quick and convenient to make. Garlic is beneficial for treating a range of complaints and has numerous therapeutic benefits, such as lowering cholesterol and blood pressure, protecting against infection, and it is believed to help to prevent some types of cancer.

Serves 4

30ml//2 tbsp olive oil
1 garlic clove, crushed
900g/2lb/8 cups frozen peas
1.2 litres/2 pints/5 cups vegetable stock
ground black pepper
fresh mint, to garnish

1 Heat the oil in a large pan and add the garlic. Fry gently for 2 minutes, then add the peas. Cook for 1–2 minutes more, then pour in the stock.

Cook's tip
If you keep a bag of frozen peas in the freezer, you can rustle up this soup at very short notice.

2 Bring the soup to the boil, then reduce the heat to a simmer. Cover and cook for 5–6 minutes, until the peas are tender. Leave to cool slightly, then transfer the mixture to a food processor and process until smooth (you may have to do this in two batches).

3 Return the soup to the pan and heat through gently. Season with pepper to taste. Serve garnished with mint.

Energy 236Kcal/977kJ; Protein 15.7g; Carbohydrate 25.4g, of which sugars 5.2g; Fat 9g, of which saturates 1.5g; Cholesterol 0mg; Calcium 48mg; Fibre 10.6g; Sodium 112mg.

Russian borscht with kvas

Beetroot is the main ingredient of this flavoursome and vibrantly coloured soup. It is a powerful blood cleanser and tonic and can aid the digestive system. It is also a good source of potassium and folate as well as iron. If you are not following a strict detox diet, you could serve this soup with a generous spoonful of creamy yogurt.

3 Add the crushed garlic and chopped tomatoes to the pan and cook, stirring, for 2 more minutes.

4 Place the bay leaf, parsley, cloves and peppercorns in a piece of muslin (cheesecloth) and tie with string.

5 Add the muslin bag to the pan with the stock. Bring to the boil, reduce the heat, cover and simmer for 1¼ hours, until the vegetables are tender. Discard the bag. Stir in the beetroot kvas and season. Ladle into bowls and serve garnished with chives or dill.

Serves 4

900g/2lb raw beetroot (beets), peeled
2 carrots, peeled
2 celery sticks
30ml/2 tbsp olive oil
2 onions, sliced
2 garlic cloves, crushed
4 tomatoes, peeled, seeded and chopped
1 bay leaf
1 large parsley sprig
2 cloves
4 whole peppercorns
1.2 litres/2 pints/5 cups chicken or
    vegetable stock
150ml/¼ pint/⅔ cup beetroot kvas
    (see Cook's Tip)
ground black pepper
chopped fresh chives or sprigs of dill,
    to garnish

1 Cut the beetroot, carrots and celery into thick strips. Heat the oil in a pan and cook the onions over a low heat for 5 minutes, stirring occasionally.

2 Add the beetroot, carrots and celery to the pan and cook for a further 5 minutes, on a low heat, stirring from time to time, until the vegetables are slightly softened.

Cook's tip
Beetroot kvas adds an intense colour and a slight tartness to the soup. Peel and grate 1 beetroot, add 150ml/¼ pint/⅔ cup stock and 10ml/2 tsp lemon juice. Bring to the boil, cover and remove from the heat. Leave for 30 minutes. Strain before using.

Energy 172Kcal/723kJ; Protein 5.1g; Carbohydrate 25.5g, of which sugars 23.5g; Fat 6.2g, of which saturates 0.9g; Cholesterol 0mg; Calcium 75mg; Fibre 6.9g; Sodium 180mg.

Spicy pumpkin soup

Pumpkins and the many varieties of winter squash, such as butternut and acorn, are a good source of betacarotene, which the body converts into vitamin A. The delicious flesh is easily digestible and rarely causes problems for those with food sensitivities. Ginger and cumin give the soup its spicy flavour and also help to aid digestion.

Serves 4

900g/2lb pumpkin, peeled and
    seeds removed
30ml/2 tbsp olive oil
2 leeks, trimmed and sliced
1 garlic clove, crushed
5ml/1 tsp ground ginger
5ml/1 tsp ground cumin
900ml/1½ pints/3¾ cups vegetable stock
ground black pepper
fresh thyme, to garnish
60ml/4 tbsp low-fat probiotic yogurt, to serve

5 Bring the soup to the boil and simmer over a low heat for about 30 minutes, until the pumpkin is tender. Process in batches, if necessary, in a blender or food processor.

6 Warm the soup through again, being careful not to bring it to the boiling point, and serve in warmed individual bowls, with a swirl of yogurt on top. Garnish with fresh thyme leaves.

Cook's tip
Add extra colour and flavour to this soup by stirring in 30ml/2 tbsp chopped fresh coriander (cilantro) leaves before serving.

1 Cut the peeled pumpkin into large chunks. Heat the olive oil in a large pan and add the sliced leeks and garlic.

2 Cook gently over a low heat until the vegetables are softened.

3 Stir in the ginger and cumin and cook, stirring, for a further minute.

4 Add the pumpkin and the vegetable stock and season with freshly ground black pepper.

Energy 101Kcal/420kJ; Protein 3.2g; Carbohydrate 7.9g, of which sugars 6g; Fat 6.5g, of which saturates 1.1g; Cholesterol 0mg; Calcium 89mg; Fibre 4.5g; Sodium 2mg.

Borlotti bean and vegetable soup

This is an Italian-style soup, rather like minestrone, but made with beans instead of pasta. It is served ladled over spinach, or other dark green leafy vegetables. You can use any type of canned beans – ideally choose those canned in water. They are wonderfully nutritious and high in dietary fibre, which is essential for healthy digestion.

Serves 4

45ml/3 tbsp olive oil
2 onions, chopped
2 carrots, sliced
4 garlic cloves, crushed
2 celery sticks, thinly sliced
1 fennel bulb, trimmed and chopped
2 large courgettes (zucchini), thinly sliced
400g/14oz can chopped tomatoes
30ml/2 tbsp home-made or bought pesto
900ml/1½ pints/3¾ cups vegetable stock
400g/14oz can borlotti or haricot (navy)
  beans, drained and rinsed
450g/1lb fresh young spinach
ground black pepper

1 Heat 30ml/2 tbsp of oil in a large pan. Add the chopped onions, carrots, crushed garlic, celery and fennel and fry gently for about 10 minutes.

2 Add the courgettes and fry for a further 2 minutes.

Variation
You can use other dark greens, such as chard or cabbage, instead of the spinach; simply shred and cook until tender, then spoon over the soup.

3 Stir in the chopped tomatoes, pesto, stock and beans and bring to the boil. Lower the heat, cover and simmer for 25–30 minutes, until the vegetables are completely tender. Season with black pepper to taste.

4 Heat the remaining oil in a frying pan and quickly stir-fry the spinach for 1 minute, just until wilted. Spoon the spinach into heated soup bowls, then ladle the soup over the spinach. Sprinkle with ground black pepper, and serve immediately.

Energy 359Kcal/1496kJ; Protein 14.3g; Carbohydrate 40.7g, of which sugars 23.4g; Fat 16.5g, of which saturates 2.5g; Cholesterol 0mg; Calcium 353mg; Fibre 15.1g; Sodium 599mg.

Butter bean, tomato and pesto soup

This soup is very quick and easy to make, and uses a combination of store-cupboard ingredients and fresh, preferably home-made, pesto and stock. You could use other types of beans as an alternative to butter beans, if you prefer. Make plenty at once and then freeze in batches so that you have some to hand as a quick meal when you are hungry after a long day.

Serves 4

2 x 400g/14oz cans butter (lima) beans, drained and rinsed
900ml/1½ pints/3¾ cups vegetable stock
60ml/4 tbsp sun-dried tomato purée (paste)
75ml/5 tbsp fresh pesto, (preferably home-made)

Cook's tip
Use a home-made or good-quality bought fresh stock for the best natural flavour. It will also be free from the additives and excess salt found in stock (bouillon) cubes.

1 Put the rinsed and drained beans in a large pan with the stock and bring just to the boil.

2 Reduce the heat and stir in the tomato purée and pesto. Cover, bring back to simmering point and cook gently for 5 minutes.

3 Transfer six ladlefuls of the soup to a blender or food processor, scooping up plenty of the beans. Process until smooth, then return to the pan.

4 Heat gently, stirring frequently, for 5 minutes, then season if necessary. Ladle into four warmed soup bowls.

Energy 255Kcal/1071kJ; Protein 14.9g; Carbohydrate 28.2g, of which sugars 4.4g; Fat 9.9g, of which saturates 2.1g; Cholesterol 5mg; Calcium 96mg; Fibre 9.7g; Sodium 931mg.

main dish salads

Tempting, nutritionally balanced salads can be made from an endless variety of ingredients, including fresh fruit and vegetables for vitamins, nuts or seeds for protein, and rice, new potatoes or beans for carbohydrate. All these delicious dishes are suitable for a weekend detox, and will satisfy both your stomach and your senses.

Red pepper and sprout salad with cashew cream dressing

This satisfying salad has contrasting colours, textures and flavours. The creamy nut dressing, which is full of protein and nutrients, transforms any salad into a wholesome meal.

Serves 1–2

115g/4oz unsalted cashew nuts
1 red (bell) pepper, seeded and diced
90g/3½ oz mung bean, aduki bean or
   chickpea sprouts
½ cucumber
juice of ½ lemon
small bunch fresh parsley, coriander
   (cilantro) or basil, finely chopped
5ml/1 tsp sesame, sunflower or
   pumpkin seeds

1 Put the cashew nuts in a heatproof bowl, pour over 100ml/3½/scant ½ cup boiling water, then leave them to soak for a few hours, preferably overnight, until softened.

2 Process the nuts with their soaking water in a food processor or blender until you have a smooth sauce. Add more water if necessary.

3 Peel away the cucumber skin in strips lengthways to produce a striped effect. Cut the cucumber into dice.

4 Place the pepper, sprouts, cucumber and lemon juice in a bowl and toss together. Serve with the cashew cream dressing and scatter with the herbs and seeds.

Health benefits

The cashew cream makes a smooth dressing that can be used for salads or as a sauce. Cashew nuts are rich in monounsaturated fatty acids, and they are favoured for their heart-protecting and anti-cancer properties.

Sprouting beans and seeds increases their nutritional value without losing any of the plant enzymes that are good for the digestive system. Sprouted beans contain vitamins A and B complex, C and E, and the vitamin content can increase by almost 200 per cent when the sprouts begin to turn green on exposure to light, due to the effect of energy-producing chlorophyll.

Cook's tips

• There are many different kinds of sprouts, and beansprouts are one of the types most readily available commercially. Rinse them in cold water before using in salads and other recipes.

• Choose fresh, crisp sprouts with the seed or bean still attached. Avoid any that are slimy or that smell musty.

• Sprouts are best eaten on the day they are bought, but, if they are fresh, they will keep for 2–3 days tightly wrapped in a plastic bag in the refrigerator.

• You can sprout most whole beans or grains yourself. Favourites include aduki, alfalfa, haricot (navy), lentils, mung, sunflower, cress and wheat sprouts. In general, the smaller beans will sprout more successfully than larger ones. Always use organic, unsprayed beans from a health food store for sprouting at home.

Energy 402Kcal/1668kJ; Protein 14.7g; Carbohydrate 18.9g, of which sugars 10.1g; Fat 30.2g, of which saturates 6g; Cholesterol 0mg; Calcium 86mg; Fibre 5.2g; Sodium 181mg.

Summer vegetable salad with hazelnuts

This nutrient-packed salad makes a perfect detox lunch or supper. Nuts supply a good source of vegetable protein, and hazelnuts in particular are rich in the antioxidant vitamin E. The combination of vegetables can be varied according to what is available when you go shopping.

Serves 4

30ml/2 tbsp olive oil
1 shallot, chopped
1 celery stick, sliced
225g/8oz assorted wild and cultivated
    mushrooms such as young ceps, shiitake
    and chanterelles, trimmed and sliced
freshly ground black pepper
175g/6oz small new potatoes, scrubbed
115g/4oz French (green) beans, trimmed
115g/4oz baby carrots, trimmed and peeled
50g/2oz baby corn, trimmed
50g/2oz asparagus spears, trimmed
115g/4oz/1 cup broad (fava) beans
30ml/2 tbsp hazelnut oil
15ml/1 tbsp vegetable oil
15ml/1 tbsp lemon juice
5ml/1 tsp chopped fresh thyme
50g/2oz hazelnuts, toasted and chopped

1 Fry the shallot and celery in olive oil until soft but without colouring. Add the mushrooms and cook over a moderate heat until their juices begin to run, then increase the heat to boil off the juices. Season with ground black pepper, then transfer to a bowl.

2 In separate steaming baskets, steam the potatoes for 20 minutes, the French beans, carrots, corn and asparagus for 6 minutes and the broad beans for 3 minutes. Cool under cold running water. Remove the tough outer skins of the broad beans, and cut the potatoes and all the vegetables in half.

3 Combine the steamed vegetables with the mushrooms, then moisten with the hazelnut and vegetable oils. Add the lemon juice and chopped thyme, season with ground black pepper and scatter the toasted hazelnuts over the top.

Health benefits

• Mushrooms are a useful souce of B vitamins as well as providing the minerals potassium and copper. Oriental mushrooms have been at the centre of much attention because of their powerful antiviral properties, which boost the immune system.
• Although hazelnuts, like all nuts, are high in calories, they provide valuable amounts of B group vitamins, vitamin E, calcium and iron, and zinc, as well as essential fatty acids – vital in a balanced diet.

Energy 295Kcal/1224kJ; Protein 7.5g; Carbohydrate 16.3g, of which sugars 5.7g; Fat 22.7g, of which saturates 2.7g; Cholesterol 0mg; Calcium 68mg; Fibre 5.8g; Sodium 166mg.

Mixed bean salad

The speckled herb, lemon and roasted red pepper dressing adds a vitamin C boost to this salad. Perfect for a detox lunch, it will provide a steady stream of energy throughout the day. You could substitute the flageolet or cannellini beans with broad beans, butter beans or pinto beans.

Serves 4

1 large red (bell) pepper
60ml/4 tbsp olive oil
1 large garlic clove, crushed
25g/1oz/1 cup fresh flat leaf parsley, basil
   or mint
15ml/1 tbsp lemon juice
400g/14oz can flageolet (pale green) beans,
   drained and rinsed
200g/7oz/1½ cups canned cannellini beans,
   drained and rinsed
ground black pepper

1 Preheat the oven to 200°C/400°F/ Gas 6. Rinse the red pepper under running water, pat dry, then place on a baking sheet, brush with a little of the olive oil and roast in the preheated oven for 15–20 minutes, or until it is wrinkled and soft.

Health benefits
Dried beans, peas and lentils are low in fat and high in fibre and protein and should be a regular part of a healthy balanced diet. They are also a good source of many minerals, including iron, zinc, potassium and magnesium, as well as B complex vitamins.
   Canned beans are quick and convenient to use. Choose those canned in water rather than brine, if possible, and rinse thoroughly before using.

2 Remove the pepper from the oven and place in a plastic bag. Seal the bag and leave to cool. (This makes the skin easier to remove.)

3 When the pepper is cool enough to handle, remove it from the bag and carefully peel off the skin. Rinse the peeled pepper under running water.

4 Slice the pepper in half and remove the seeds and stem, gently using a knife to scrape away the membrane that holds the seeds in place. Dice the pepper, retaining any juices. Set aside.

5 Heat the remaining olive oil in a pan and cook the garlic for about 1 minute until softened. Remove from the heat, then add the herbs, the roasted red pepper and any retained juices, and the lemon juice. Stir together gently to combine thoroughly.

6 Put the flageolet and cannellini beans in a large serving bowl and pour over the dressing. Season to taste, then stir gently until well combined. Serve the salad warm or cold.

Energy 265Kcal/1110kJ; Protein 11g; Carbohydrate 29.7g, of which sugars 8.2g; Fat 12.2g, of which saturates 1.8g; Cholesterol 0mg; Calcium 123mg; Fibre 10.3g; Sodium 589mg.

Avocado, red onion and spinach salad

The simple lemon dressing gives a sharp tang to the creamy avocado, sweet, roasted red onions and crisp, fresh spinach. Golden polenta croûtons provide a delicious wheat-free alternative to bread croûtons and make this light salad more sustaining. You could use other fresh salad leaves, such as rocket or watercress, in place of the spinach, if you like.

Serves 4

1 large red onion, cut into wedges
300g/11oz ready-made polenta, cut into
    1cm/½in cubes
olive oil, for brushing
225g/8oz baby spinach leaves
1 avocado, peeled, stoned and sliced
5ml/1 tsp lemon juice

For the dressing
60ml/4 tbsp extra virgin olive oil
juice of ½ lemon
ground black pepper

1 Preheat the oven to 200°C/400°F/
Gas 6.

2 Place the red onion wedges and polenta cubes on a lightly oiled baking sheet and bake in the preheated oven for 25 minutes, or until the onion is tender and the polenta is crisp and golden, turning them regularly to prevent them sticking.

3 Turn the onions and polenta cubes on to kitchen paper and leave to cool.

4 Meanwhile, make the dressing for the salad. Place the olive oil, lemon juice and pepper to taste in a bowl or screw-top jar. Stir or shake thoroughly to combine.

5 Place the baby spinach leaves in a serving bowl. Toss the avocado slices in the lemon juice to prevent them from browning, then add to the spinach with the roasted onions.

6 Pour the dressing over the salad and toss gently to combine. Sprinkle the polenta croûtons on top of the salad or hand them round separately, and serve immediately.

Health benefits
Avocados have been traditionally regarded as a high-fat food that should be avoided. However, although they do contain high amounts of fat, it is beneficial monounsaturated fat, and research has revealed that this type of fat can help to decrease the level of cholesterol in the blood. Avocados also have a valuable vitamin and mineral content, and eating them can help to improve the condition of your skin and hair.

Energy 445Kcal/1849kJ; Protein 8.1g; Carbohydrate 48.3g, of which sugars 1.8g; Fat 23.9g, of which saturates 3.5g; Cholesterol 0mg; Calcium 104mg; Fibre 3.6g; Sodium 81mg.

Mushroom rice with cashew nuts

This sustaining warm rice salad combines earthy mushrooms, spicy chillies, fragrant coriander and golden cashew nuts to create a delicious dish that is suitable for lunch or dinner. A wide range of organic mushrooms is readily available. They combine well with rice and garlic chives to make a tasty accompaniment to vegetarian dishes, fish or chicken.

Serves 4

350g/12oz/generous 1¾ cups long
  grain rice
60ml/4 tbsp vegetable oil
1 small onion, finely chopped
2 fresh green chillies, seeded and
  finely chopped
25g/1oz chives, chopped
15g/½oz fresh coriander (cilantro)
600ml/1 pint/2½ cups vegetable stock
250g/9oz mixed mushrooms, thickly sliced
2 garlic cloves, crushed
50g/2oz unsalted cashew nuts
ground black pepper

1 Wash and drain the rice. Heat half the oil in a large pan and cook the onion and chillies over a gentle heat, stirring occasionally, for 10–12 minutes until softened.

2 Set half the chives aside. Cut the stalks off the coriander and set the leaves aside. Blend the remaining chives and the coriander stalks with the stock in a food processor or blender.

3 Add the rice to the onions and stir-fry over a low heat for 4–5 minutes. Pour in the herb stock, then stir in a good grinding of black pepper.

4 Bring to the boil, then stir and reduce the heat to very low. Cover tightly with a lid and cook for 15–20 minutes, or until the rice has absorbed all the liquid.

5 Remove the pan from the heat and lay a clean, folded dish towel over the pan, under the lid, and press on the lid to wedge it firmly in place.

6 Leave the rice to stand for a further 10 minutes, allowing the towel to absorb the steam while the rice becomes completely tender.

7 Meanwhile, heat the remaining oil and cook the mushrooms for 3–4 minutes. Add the remaining chives and cook for another 1–2 minutes.

8 Stir the garlic mushrooms into the rice and add the reserved coriander leaves. Adjust the seasoning to taste, then transfer to a serving dish and serve immediately, sprinkled with the toasted cashew nuts.

Variation
For a higher-fibre alternative use brown rice. Increase the cooking time in Step 3 to 25–30 minutes. Add extra stock as needed.

Energy 507Kcal/2112kJ; Protein 10.7g; Carbohydrate 74g, of which sugars 2g; Fat 18.3g, of which saturates 2.9g; Cholesterol 0mg; Calcium 54mg; Fibre 1.9g; Sodium 44mg.

vegetable main dishes

Take advantage of the wide variety of cereal grains, beans, peas, lentils, and vegetables to make wholesome and satisfying meals, such as Harvest Vegetable and Lentil Casserole, Stir-fried Rice and Vegetables or Mixed Bean and Aubergine Tagine with Mint Yogurt. These are ideal for a detox diet as they are packed with nutrients, are filling to eat and are easily digested, as well as being suitable for vegetarians. Flavour the dishes with fresh herbs and spices, which aid the digestion.

Spanish-style vegetables with thyme

This recipe includes courgettes, fennel, onion, peppers, butternut squash and tomatoes, but you can use any combination you like. Cooking the vegetables in this way brings out their flavour magnificently, and the addition of the fresh thyme and a sprinkling of cumin seeds further enhances their flavour and negates the need for added salt.

Serves 4

2–3 courgettes (zucchini)
1 large fennel bulb
1 Spanish (Bermuda) onion
2 large red (bell) peppers
450g/1lb butternut squash
6 whole garlic cloves, unpeeled
60ml/4 tbsp olive oil
juice of ½ lemon
pinch of cumin seeds, crushed
4 sprigs fresh thyme
4 medium tomatoes
ground black pepper

1 Preheat the oven to 220°C/425°F/Gas 7. Cut all the vegetables into large bitesize pieces. Smash the garlic with the flat of a knife, but leave the skins on.

2 Choose a large roasting pan into which all the vegetables will fit in one layer. Put in all the vegetables except the tomatoes.

3 Mix together the oil and lemon juice. Pour over the vegetables and toss them. Sprinkle with the cumin seeds and pepper and tuck in the thyme sprigs. Roast for 20 minutes.

4 Gently turn the vegetables in the oil and add the tomatoes. Cook for a further 15 minutes, or until tender and slightly charred around the edges.

Variations

• This is a very easy, pretty dish to make and you can vary the choice of vegetables according to what is available and in season. Baby vegetables such as leeks and courgettes (zucchini) are excellent roasted. Judge the roasting time by their size. Wedges of red onion or whole shallots would also be good.
• Aubergines (eggplant) are frequently included in this mixture, and their flavour is delicious, but they turn a slightly unappetizing grey colour when cooked and served plain.
• Fresh rosemary sprigs could be used in place of the fresh thyme, if you like.

Energy 213Kcal/883kJ; Protein 5.7g; Carbohydrate 20.3g, of which sugars 17.5g; Fat 12.6g, of which saturates 2g; Cholesterol 0mg; Calcium 109mg; Fibre 7.3g; Sodium 24mg.

Roasted vegetables with salsa verde

There are endless variations of the Italian salsa verde, which means "green sauce". Usually a blend of fresh chopped herbs, garlic, olive oil, anchovies and capers, this is a simplified version. Here, it is served with a variety of roasted vegetables and rice. The herbs, mint and parsley, both help to aid the digestion and to prevent garlic breath.

Serves 4

3 courgettes (zucchini), sliced lengthways
1 large fennel bulb, cut into wedges
450g/1lb butternut squash, cut into
   2cm/¾in chunks
12 shallots
2 red (bell) peppers, seeded and cut
   lengthways into thick slices
4 plum tomatoes, halved and seeded
45ml/3 tbsp olive oil
2 garlic cloves, crushed
5ml/1 tsp balsamic vinegar
ground black pepper

For the salsa verde
45ml/3 tbsp chopped fresh mint
90ml/6 tbsp chopped fresh flat leaf parsley
15ml/1 tbsp Dijon mustard
juice of ½ lemon
30ml/2 tbsp olive oil

For the rice
15ml/1 tbsp vegetable or olive oil
75g/3oz/¾ cup vermicelli, broken into short
   lengths (optional)
225g/8oz/generous 1 cup long grain rice
900ml/1½ pints/3¾ cups vegetable stock

1 Preheat the oven to 220°C/425°F/ Gas 7. To make the salsa verde, place all the ingredients, with the exception of the olive oil, in a food processor or blender. Blend to a coarse paste, then add the oil, a little at a time, until the mixture forms a smooth purée. Season to taste.

2 To roast the vegetables, toss the courgettes, fennel, squash, shallots, peppers and tomatoes in the olive oil, garlic and balsamic vinegar. Leave to stand for 10 minutes to allow the flavours to mingle.

3 Place all the vegetables – apart from the squash and tomatoes – in a large roasting pan, brush with half the oil and vinegar mixture and season.

4 Roast for 20 minutes, then remove from the oven. Turn the vegetables over and brush with the rest of the oil and vinegar mixture. Add the squash and tomatoes and cook for a further 15–20 minutes until all the vegetables are tender and lightly blackened around the edges.

5 Meanwhile, prepare the rice. Heat the oil in a heavy pan. Add the vermicelli, if using, and fry for about 3 minutes, or until golden and crisp.

6 Rinse the rice under cold running water, then drain well and stir it into the vermicelli. Add the vegetable stock, then cover and cook for 12 minutes until the water is absorbed. Stir the rice, then cover and leave to stand for 10 minutes. Serve with the roasted vegetables and salsa verde.

Cook's tip
The salsa verde will keep for up to 1 week if it is stored in an airtight container in the refrigerator.

Energy 556Kcal/2314kJ; Protein 13.3g; Carbohydrate 83.5g, of which sugars 20.5g; Fat 18.9g, of which saturates 2.8g; Cholesterol 0mg; Calcium 173mg; Fibre 9.3g; Sodium 34mg.

Harvest vegetable and lentil casserole

Take advantage of a wide range of fresh root vegetables when they are in season in order to produce a delicious hearty dish that's full of natural goodness. Lentils are a nutritional superfood – high in protein, starchy carbohydrate and fibre, but very low in sodium and fat. Serve with brown rice, if liked, for a more substantial meal.

Serves 6

15ml/1 tbsp vegetable oil
2 leeks, diagonally sliced
1 garlic clove, crushed
4 celery sticks, diagonally sliced
2 carrots, diagonally sliced
2 parsnips, diced
1 sweet potato, diced
225g/8oz swede (rutabaga), diced
175g/6oz whole brown or green lentils
450g/1lb tomatoes, skinned, seeded
　　and chopped
15ml/1 tbsp chopped fresh thyme
15ml/1 tbsp chopped fresh marjoram
900ml/1½ pints/3¾ cups vegetable stock
15ml/1 tbsp cornflour (cornstarch)
ground black pepper
sprigs of fresh thyme, to garnish

1 Preheat the oven to 180°C/350°F/Gas 4. Heat the oil in a flameproof casserole over a moderate heat. Add the leeks, garlic and celery and cook gently for 3 minutes.

2 Add the carrots, parsnips, sweet potato, swede, lentils, tomatoes, herbs, stock and pepper to taste. Stir well. Bring to the boil, stirring occasionally.

3 Cover the casserole and bake in the oven for about 50 minutes, until the vegetables and the lentils are cooked and tender. During the cooking time, remove the casserole from the oven and stir the vegetable mixture once or twice so that it is evenly cooked.

4 Remove the casserole from the oven. Blend the cornflour with 45ml/3 tbsp cold water in a bowl. Stir into the casserole and heat on the stove, stirring continuously, until the mixture comes to the boil and thickens. Simmer gently for 2 minutes.

5 Spoon the vegetable mixture into warm bowls and serve immediately, garnished with thyme sprigs.

Cook's tip
Although lentils keep well, they toughen with time. Buy from shops with a fast turnover of stock and store them in airtight containers.

Energy 202Kcal/857kJ; Protein 9.4g; Carbohydrate 36.2g, of which sugars 10.3g; Fat 3.2g, of which saturates 0.5g; Cholesterol 0mg; Calcium 70mg; Fibre 6.3g; Sodium 60mg.

Spring vegetable stir-fry

Fast, fresh and packed with healthy vegetables, this stir-fry makes an ideal supper dish. Serve it with rice during a wheat-free detox or noodles during a less strict regime. Stir-fries are best flavoured with garlic and ginger, both of which have a distinctive flavour and are great detox spices, helping to stimulate and aid the digestive system.

Serves 4

15ml/1 tbsp vegetable oil
5ml/1 tsp toasted sesame oil
1 garlic clove, chopped
2.5cm/1in piece fresh root ginger,
  finely chopped
225g/8oz baby carrots
350g/12oz broccoli florets
175g/6oz asparagus tips
2 spring onions (scallions), diagonally sliced
175g/6oz/1½ cups spring greens, (collards)
  finely shredded
30ml/2 tbsp soy sauce
15ml/1 tbsp fresh apple juice
15ml/1 tbsp sesame seeds, toasted
rice or noodles, to serve

1 Heat a large frying pan or wok over a high heat. Add the vegetable oil and the sesame oil, and reduce the heat. Add the garlic and sauté gently for 2 minutes.

2 Add the ginger, baby carrots, broccoli and asparagus tips to the pan and stir-fry for about 4 minutes. Add the spring onions and spring greens to the pan and stir-fry for a further 2 minutes.

3 Add the soy sauce and apple juice and cook for 1–2 minutes until the vegetables are tender, adding a little water if they appear dry.

4 Spoon the vegetables into four warmed bowls and sprinkle with toasted sesame seeds. Serve immediately with rice or noodles.

Cook's tip
Look out for reduced-salt soy sauce. Soy sauce is quite high in sodium, so there is no need to add extra salt for seasoning.

Energy 134Kcal/554kJ; Protein 7.8g; Carbohydrate 9.4g, of which sugars 8.6g; Fat 7.4g, of which saturates 1.1g; Cholesterol 0mg; Calcium 195mg; Fibre 6.2g; Sodium 566mg.

Stir-fried rice and vegetables

The ginger and garlic combine with the array of fresh vegetables to give this flavoursome stir-fry a wonderful aroma, with the added benefit that they boost the dish's therapeutic properties. It's less usual to use brown rice for an Oriental-style dish, but this variety increases the fibre content of the meal significantly and so is worth including.

3 Slice the mushrooms, discarding the stems. Heat the vegetable oil in a wok and stir-fry the carrots for 4–5 minutes until they just start to become tender.

4 Add the mushrooms and baby courgettes and stir-fry for about 3 minutes. Add the broccoli and spring onions and stir-fry for a further 3 minutes, by which time all the vegetables should be tender but still retain a slight "bite".

5 Add the cooked rice to the wok, and toss briefly with the vegetables over the heat to combine well and heat through thoroughly.

6 Sprinkle over the soy sauce and the toasted sesame oil and toss again lightly. Spoon into individual bowls and serve immediately.

Serves 2

115g/4oz/generous ½ cup brown basmati rice, rinsed and drained
350ml/12fl oz/1½ cups vegetable stock
2.5cm/1in piece of fresh root ginger, finely sliced
1 garlic clove, halved
5cm/2in piece of pared lemon rind
115g/4oz/1½ cups shiitake mushrooms
30ml/2 tbsp vegetable oil
175g/6oz baby carrots, trimmed
225g/8oz baby courgettes (zucchini), halved
175–225g/6–8oz broccoli, broken into florets
6 spring onions (scallions), diagonally sliced
15ml/1 tbsp soy sauce
10ml/2 tsp toasted sesame oil

1 Put the brown rice in a pan and pour in the vegetable stock. Add the root ginger, garlic and lemon rind. Slowly bring to the boil, then cover the pan with a lid and cook very gently for 20–25 minutes until the rice is tender.

2 Drain and remove the ginger, garlic and lemon rind from the rice. Return the rice to the pan and cover with a lid to keep warm. Set aside.

Health benefits

• Ginger has long been recognized as an excellent detoxifier. It can provide relief for gastro-intestinal disorders, aid indigestion and help to boost the immune system.
• The starch in brown rice is absorbed slowly by the body, helping to keep blood sugar levels on an even keel, which is very important during a detox. Brown rice is also good for treating digestive disorders, soothing and cleansing the intestinal tract, calming the nervous system and preventing kidney stones.
• All vegetables are highly nutritious and a healthy diet should include at least five portions a day. Broccoli, in particular, is a very good source of vitamins C and E, and betacarotene, and provides folate.

Energy 430Kcal/1788kJ; Protein 12.5g; Carbohydrate 58.2g, of which sugars 11.2g; Fat 16.2g, of which saturates 2.2g; Cholesterol 0mg; Calcium 127mg; Fibre 6.5g; Sodium 569mg.

Thai vegetable curry

Fragrant jasmine rice, subtly flavoured with lemon grass and cardamom, is the perfect accompaniment to this spiced vegetable curry, which combines new potatoes, baby corn, broccoli, red pepper and spinach in a scented coconut milk broth. Don't be put off by the long list of ingredients – this curry is very simple to make.

Serves 4

10ml/2 tsp vegetable oil
400ml/14fl oz/1⅔ cups reduced-fat
  coconut milk
300ml/½ pint/1¼ cups vegetable stock
225g/8oz new potatoes, halved or quartered,
  if large
130g/4½oz baby corn
5ml/1 tsp caster (superfine) sugar
200g/7oz broccoli florets
1 red (bell) pepper, seeded and
  sliced lengthways
115g/4oz spinach, tough stalks removed
  and shredded
30ml/2 tbsp chopped fresh coriander (cilantro)
ground black pepper

For the spice paste

1 fresh red chilli, seeded and chopped
3 fresh green chillies, seeded and chopped
1 lemon grass stalk, outer leaves removed
  and lower 5cm/2in finely chopped
2 shallots, chopped
finely grated rind of 1 lime
2 garlic cloves, chopped
5ml/1 tsp ground coriander
2.5ml/½ tsp ground cumin
1cm/½in fresh galangal or root ginger,
  finely chopped
30ml/2 tbsp chopped fresh coriander (cilantro)

For the rice

225g/8oz/generous 1 cup jasmine rice, rinsed
1 lemon grass stalk, outer leaves removed
  and cut into 3 pieces
6 cardamom pods, bruised

1 Make the spice paste. Place all the ingredients in a food processor or blender and blend to a coarse paste.

2 Heat the oil in a large, heavy pan and fry the spice paste for 1–2 minutes, stirring constantly. Add the coconut milk and stock to the pan, and bring to the boil.

3 Reduce the heat, add the potatoes and simmer for 15 minutes. Add the baby corn, then cook for 2 minutes. Stir in the sugar, broccoli and red pepper, and cook for 2 minutes more until the vegetables are tender. Stir in the shredded spinach and half the fresh coriander. Cook for 2 minutes.

4 Meanwhile, prepare the rice. Put the rinsed rice into a large pan and add the prepared lemon grass and cardamom pods. Pour over 475ml/16fl oz/2 cups cold water.

5 Bring to the boil, then reduce the heat, cover, and cook for 10–15 minutes until the water is absorbed and the rice is tender and slightly sticky. Season to taste with pepper, leave to stand for 10 minutes, then fluff up the rice with a fork.

6 Remove the lemon grass and cardomom pods and serve the rice with the curry, sprinkled with the remaining chopped fresh coriander.

Energy 327Kcal/1374kJ; Protein 9.9g; Carbohydrate 64.8g, of which sugars 11.1g; Fat 3.3g, of which saturates 0.6g; Cholesterol 0mg; Calcium 134mg; Fibre 3.9g; Sodium 534mg.

Barley risotto with roasted squash and leeks

This is more like a pilaff made with slightly chewy, nutty-flavoured pearl barley than a classic risotto. Sweet leeks and roasted butternut squash are superb with this earthy grain.

Serves 4

200g/7oz/1 cup pearl barley
1 butternut squash, peeled, seeded and
    cut into chunks
10ml/2 tsp chopped fresh thyme
60ml/4 tbsp olive oil
4 leeks, cut into fairly thick
    diagonal slices
2 garlic cloves, finely chopped
175g/6oz/2½ cups brown cap (cremini)
    mushrooms, sliced
2 carrots, coarsely grated
about 120ml/4fl oz/½ cup vegetable stock
30ml/2 tbsp chopped fresh flat
    leaf parsley
45ml/3 tbsp pumpkin seeds, toasted,
    or chopped walnuts
ground black pepper

1 Rinse the barley, then cook it in simmering water, keeping the pan part-covered, for 35–45 minutes, or until tender. Drain. Preheat the oven to 200°C/400°F/Gas 6.

2 Put the squash in a roasting pan with half the thyme. Season with pepper and toss with half the oil. Roast for 30 minutes, stirring once, until the squash is tender.

3 Heat the remaining olive oil in a large frying pan. Cook the leeks and garlic gently for 5 minutes. Add the mushrooms and remaining thyme, then cook until the liquid from the mushrooms evaporates and they begin to fry.

4 Stir in the carrots and cook for about 2 minutes, then add the barley and most of the vegetable stock. Season well and part-cover the pan. Cook for a further 5 minutes. Pour in the remaining stock if the mixture seems dry.

5 Stir in the roasted squash and the parsley. Add seasoning to taste and serve immediately, sprinkled with the toasted pumpkin seeds or walnuts.

Variations

• Make the risotto with brown rice instead of the pearl barley, if you prefer. Cook the rice according to the packet instructions and continue from Step 2.
• Any type of mushrooms can be used in this recipe – try sliced field (portabello) mushrooms for a hearty, earthy flavour.
• For those not following a strict detox and avoiding dairy products, a little grated parmesan cheese can be stirred through the risotto or sprinkled over before serving.

Energy 398Kcal/1670kJ; Protein 9.1g; Carbohydrate 52.8g, of which sugars 7.7g; Fat 18.1g, of which saturates 2.4g; Cholesterol 0mg; Calcium 121mg; Fibre 5g; Sodium 21mg.

Vegetable couscous with olives and almonds

Couscous is a light, fluffy grain that's low in fat and high in good starchy carbohydrate. It doesn't require cooking, just soaking – making this an easy lunch or supper dish.

Serves 4

275g/10oz/1⅔ cups couscous
525ml/18fl oz/2¼ cups boiling
  vegetable stock
16–20 black olives
2 small courgettes (zucchini)
25g/1oz/¼ cup flaked (sliced)
  almonds, toasted
60ml/4 tbsp olive oil
15ml/1 tbsp lemon juice
15ml/1 tbsp chopped fresh coriander (cilantro)
15ml/1 tbsp chopped fresh parsley
good pinch of ground cumin
good pinch of paprika

3 Add the courgette strips, black olives and toasted almonds to the bowl of couscous and gently mix together to combine thoroughly.

4 Blend together the olive oil, lemon juice, herbs and spices. Pour the dressing over the couscous. Gently stir to combine, and serve.

1 Place the couscous in a heatproof bowl and pour over the boiling vegetable stock. Stir with a fork to combine, then set aside for 10 minutes. When the stock has been absorbed, fluff the grains with a fork.

2 Meanwhile, halve the olives and discard the stones (pits). Top and tail the courgettes and cut into matchsticks.

Variations

• Add extra flavour to this salad by stirring in 10ml/2 tsp grated fresh root ginger.
• Couscous is made from semolina and is therefore a wheat product. For a wheat-free alternative, substitute brown rice or quinoa.

Energy 319Kcal/1326kJ; Protein 6.6g; Carbohydrate 36.9g, of which sugars 1.4g; Fat 16.9g, of which saturates 2.1g; Cholesterol 0mg; Calcium 73mg; Fibre 1.9g; Sodium 287mg.

Mixed bean and aubergine tagine with mint yogurt

In this satisfying Moroccan dish, a mixture of red kidney and black-eyed beans with aubergine provide both texture and flavour, and are enhanced by the herbs and chillies.

Serves 4

115g/4oz/generous ½ cup dried red kidney beans, soaked overnight in cold water and drained
115g/4oz/generous ½ cup dried black-eyed beans (peas) or cannellini beans, soaked overnight in cold water and drained
600ml/1 pint/2½ cups water
2 bay leaves
2 celery sticks, each cut into 4 matchsticks
60ml/4 tbsp olive oil
1 aubergine (eggplant), about 350g/12oz, cut into chunks
1 onion, thinly sliced
3 garlic cloves, crushed
1–2 fresh red chillies, seeded and chopped
30ml/2 tbsp tomato purée (paste)
5ml/1 tsp paprika
2 large tomatoes, roughly chopped
300ml/½ pint/1¼ cups vegetable stock
15ml/1 tbsp each chopped fresh mint, parsley and coriander (cilantro)
ground black pepper
fresh herb sprigs, to garnish

For the mint yogurt
150ml/¼ pint/⅔ cup low-fat probiotic yogurt
30ml/2 tbsp chopped fresh mint
2 spring onions (scallions), chopped

1 Place the kidney beans in a large pan of unsalted boiling water. Bring back to the boil and cook for 10 minutes. Drain.

2 Place the soaked and drained black-eyed or cannellini beans in a separate large pan of boiling unsalted water and boil rapidly for 10 minutes, then drain.

3 Place the 600ml/1 pint/2½ cups of water in a large tagine or casserole, and add the bay leaves, celery and beans. Cover and place in an unheated oven. Set the oven to 190°C/375°F/Gas 5. Cook for 1–1½ hours or until the beans are tender, then drain.

4 Heat 45ml/3 tbsp of the oil in a large frying pan or cast-iron tagine base. Add the aubergine chunks and cook, stirring for 4–5 minutes until evenly browned. Remove and set aside, on a plate.

5 Add the remaining oil to the tagine base or frying pan, then add the sliced onion and cook, stirring, for about 4–5 minutes, until softened.

6 Add the crushed garlic and seeded, chopped red chillies and cook for a further 5 minutes, stirring frequently, until the onion is lightly golden.

7 Reset the oven temperature to 160°C/325°F/Gas 3. Add the tomato purée and paprika to the onion mixture and cook for 1–2 minutes.

8 Add the chopped tomatoes, the pan-fried chunks of aubergine, all the cooked beans and the vegetable stock to the pan, then season to taste with freshly ground black pepper.

9 Cover the tagine base with the lid or, if using a frying pan, transfer the contents to a clay tagine or casserole. Place in the oven and leave to cook for 1 hour.

10 Meanwhile, mix together the yogurt, mint and spring onions in a small serving bowl. Cover and keep chilled.

11 Just before serving, add the fresh mint, parsley and coriander to the tagine and lightly mix through the vegetables. Garnish with fresh herb sprigs and serve with the mint yogurt.

Energy 209Kcal/890kJ; Protein 16.6g; Carbohydrate 33.9g, of which sugars 9.4g; Fat 1.9g, of which saturates 0.5g; Cholesterol 1mg; Calcium 173mg; Fibre 12.3g; Sodium 62mg.

Braised beans and lentils

You can use any combination of beans to make this simple yet nourishing dish. Just remember that if you are using dried beans, they need to be soaked overnight to ensure that they will cook evenly and relatively quickly. The lentils do not need soaking. For a variation, pearl barley or brown rice could be used in place of the lentils.

Serves 4

150g/5oz/¾ cup mixed dried beans
75g/3oz/⅔ cup brown or green lentils
45ml/3 tbsp olive oil
1 large onion, finely chopped
2 garlic cloves, crushed
5 or 6 fresh sage leaves, chopped
juice of 1 lemon
3 spring onions (scallions),
   thinly sliced
60ml/4 tbsp chopped fresh dill
ground black pepper

1 Put the beans in a large bowl and cover with cold water. Leave to soak at room temperature for at least 6 hours, or preferably overnight.

2 Drain and rinse the beans, put in a large pan. Cover with cold water, bring to the boil, and cook for 1 hour. Add the lentils and cook for a further 30 minutes, until the beans and lentils are tender. Drain, reserving the cooking liquid. Return the beans and lentils to the pan.

3 Heat the oil in a frying pan and fry the onion until light golden. Add the garlic and sage, cook for 30 seconds, add the mixture to the beans, then stir in the reserved liquid and simmer for 15 minutes. Stir in the lemon juice and season to taste. Serve topped with a sprinkling of spring onions and dill.

Energy 286Kcal/1204kJ; Protein 14.8g; Carbohydrate 38.2g, of which sugars 6.1g; Fat 9.3g, of which saturates 1.3g; Cholesterol 0mg; Calcium 75mg; Fibre 4.6g; Sodium 27mg.

Giant beans baked with tomatoes

Gigantes are a type of white bean originating in Greece. They resemble butter beans but are larger, rounder and much sweeter in flavour. They make a delicious, filling dish when combined with Mediterranean flavours, such as tomatoes, onion, garlic, parsley, thyme and oregano. Serve with a green vegetable side dish or leafy salad for a warming main meal.

Serves 4

400g/14oz/1¾ cups fasolia gigantes
    or similar large dried white beans
45ml/3 tbsp olive oil
2 or 3 onions, total weight about
    300g/11oz, chopped
1 celery stick, thinly sliced
2 carrots, peeled and cubed
3 garlic cloves, thinly sliced
5ml/1 tsp each dried oregano and thyme
400g/14oz can chopped tomatoes
30ml/2 tbsp tomato purée (paste) diluted
    in 300ml/½ pint/1¼ cups hot water
2.5ml/½ tsp sugar
45ml/3 tbsp finely chopped flat
    leaf parsley
ground black pepper

1 Place the beans in a large bowl, cover with plenty of cold water, then leave to soak overnight. The next day, drain the beans, then rinse them under cold water and drain again.

2 Tip the beans into a large pan, pour in plenty of cold water to cover, then bring to the boil. Cover the pan and cook the beans until they are almost tender. Gigantes are not like other beans – they cook quickly, so keep testing them after they have been cooking for 30–40 minutes. They should not be allowed to disintegrate through overcooking.

3 When the beans are cooked, tip them into a colander or sieve (strainer) to drain, discarding the cooking liquid, and set them aside. Preheat the oven to 180°C/350°F/Gas 4.

Cook's tip
Never add salt to dried beans, peas or lentils before they are cooked, as it will make their skins leathery and tough. Season to taste after cooking and only add salt if it is needed. Always taste beans during cooking to ensure that you don't overcook them.

4 Heat the olive oil in the clean pan, add the chopped onions and sauté until light golden. Add the celery, carrots, garlic and dried herbs and stir with a wooden spatula until the garlic becomes aromatic.

5 Stir in the tomatoes, cover and cook for 10 minutes. Pour in the diluted tomato purée, then return the beans to the pan. Stir in the sugar and half the parsley, and season with pepper.

6 Transfer the bean mixture into a large baking dish and bake for 30 minutes, checking the beans once or twice and adding more hot water if they look dry. They should just be moist. Stir in the remaining parsley and serve.

Energy 437Kcal/1844kJ; Protein 25.3g; Carbohydrate 64.7g, of which sugars 19.4g; Fat 10.4g, of which saturates 1.5g; Cholesterol 0mg; Calcium 163mg; Fibre 20.3g; Sodium 67mg.

simple salads
and
side dishes

Eating plenty of vegetables is an essential part of any healthy diet, and having a good proportion of them raw, in salads, ensures that they retain their maximum nutritional value. The recipes in this chapter include a selection of hot and cold vegetable, potato and bean ideas to serve as accompaniments. Alternatively, dishes could be combined to make up a vitamin-packed meal, ideal for a detox regime and providing a healthy option for the entire family.

Grilled potatoes with chive dressing

There is something very enjoyable about using edible flowering plants and herbs from the garden. This new potato salad includes both the chive stems and the flower heads in the dressing, which is tossed into potates that have been chargrilled on a barbecue. It's served with grilled cherry tomatoes alongside. Both potatoes and tomatoes are a good source of vitamin C.

Serves 4–6

900g/2lb salad potatoes, such as charlottes,
   Jersey royals or French ratte
15ml/1 tbsp cider vinegar
90ml/6 tbsp olive oil
45ml/3 tbsp chopped chives
about 10 chive flowers
4–6 small bunches yellow cherry tomatoes
   on the vine
ground black pepper

1 Prepare the barbecue. Boil the potatoes in a large pan of lightly salted water for about 10 minutes, or until just tender. Meanwhile make the dressing by whisking the vinegar with 60ml/4 tbsp of the oil, then stirring in the chives and flowers. Drain the potatoes and cut them in half horizontally. Season to taste.

2 Once the flames have died down, position a grill rack over the coals so that it can heat up.

3 Toss the potatoes in the remaining oil and lay them on the hot grill rack, cut side down. Leave for about 5 minutes, then turn the potatoes over and cook the second side for about 3 minutes.

4 Place the potatoes in a bowl, pour over the dressing and toss to mix.

5 Grill the tomatoes for 3 minutes, or until they are just beginning to blister. Serve with the potatoes, which can be hot, warm or cold.

Energy 215Kcal/902kJ; Protein 3g; Carbohydrate 26.2g, of which sugars 4g; Fat 11.6g, of which saturates 1.8g; Cholesterol 0mg; Calcium 14mg; Fibre 2.2g; Sodium 23mg.

Asparagus and orange salad

A slightly unusual combination of ingredients with a simple dressing based on good quality fruity olive oil. Tender spears of asparagus, juicy oranges and ripe tomatoes all provide valuable amounts of vitamin C, and asparagus is also a well-known diuretic and can help to relieve fluid retention. It is also a mild laxative and may help to relieve indigestion.

Serves 4

225g/8oz asparagus, trimmed and cut into
    5cm/2in lengths
2 large oranges
2 flavoursome tomatoes, cut into eighths
50g/2oz cos or romaine lettuce leaves
30ml/2 tbsp extra-virgin olive oil
2.5ml/½ tsp sherry vinegar or balsamic vinegar
ground black pepper

1 Cook the asparagus in boiling, lightly salted water for 3–4 minutes, until just tender. The cooking time may vary according to the size of the asparagus stems. Drain and refresh under cold water, then leave on one side to cool.

4 Mix together the oil and vinegar, and add 15ml/1 tbsp of the reserved orange juice and 5ml/1 tsp of the grated rind. Season with salt and pepper. Just before serving, pour the dressing over the salad and mix gently to coat all the ingredients.

2 Finely grate the rind from half an orange and reserve. Peel both the oranges and cut into segments. Squeeze the juice from the membrane and reserve.

3 Put the asparagus, orange segments, tomatoes and lettuce into a salad bowl.

Cook's tip
The bottom of the asparagus stalk is usually hard and woody, so it will probably need to be cut off with a sharp knife. However, if you are using short, slender stems, sometimes called "spruce", then trimming may not be necessary.

Energy 102Kcal/424kJ; Protein 2.9g; Carbohydrate 9.3g, of which sugars 9.2g; Fat 6.1g, of which saturates 0.9g; Cholesterol 0mg; Calcium 58mg; Fibre 2.9g; Sodium 9mg.

Grated beetroot and celery salad

This simple salad contains beetroot and celery, both of which are effective and well documented detoxifiers. Celery, in particular, is favoured by advocates of detoxing as it contains very few calories and is recognized as being a diuretic and laxative. Be sure to use fresh raw beetroot and not the type that is preserved in vinegar.

Serves 4

450g/1lb raw beetroot (beets), peeled
  and grated
4 celery sticks, finely chopped
30ml/2 tbsp freshly squeezed apple juice
fresh herbs, to garnish

For the dressing
45ml/3 tbsp olive oil
15ml/1 tbsp cider vinegar
4 spring onions (scallions), finely sliced
30ml/2 tbsp chopped fresh parsley
ground black pepper

1 Put the grated beetroot in a large bowl. Add the chopped celery and freshly squeezed apple juice and toss everything together to mix well.

2 Put all the ingredients for the dressing in a small bowl and whisk together with a fork until well blended. Stir half of the dressing into the beetroot and celery mixture.

3 Drizzle the remaining dressing over the top of the salad. Allow to marinate for at least 2 hours before serving, for the fullest flavour.

4 Serve garnished with fresh herbs and season with more pepper, if liked.

Variation
Make a lemony dressing: substitute freshly squeezed lemon juice for the cider vinegar in the dressing. Lemon juice is a powerful astringent and cleanser and will help to stimulate the liver.

Health benefits
Beetroot's naturally rich supply of betacarotene, vitamin C, calcium and iron is at its highest when the vegetable is eaten raw. Malic and tartaric acid, found in apples, boost the digestion and help to remove impurities from the liver. Herbs are particularly beneficial during a detox as they can stimulate and cleanse the system.

Energy 123Kcal/512kJ; Protein 2.3g; Carbohydrate 9.9g, of which sugars 9.2g; Fat 8.5g, of which saturates 1.2g; Cholesterol 0mg; Calcium 42mg; Fibre 2.7g; Sodium 98mg.

Leafy salad with apple and beetroot

Crisp apple, red salad leaves and cooked beetroot combine to make this a super-cleansing salad. Both apples and beetroot are excellent for removing impurities from the liver. Red fruits and vegetables have high levels of vitamins C and E and betacarotene. These antioxidants can help to fight cell damage caused by harmful free radicals.

Serves 4

50g/2oz/⅓ cup whole unblanched almonds
2 red apples, cored and diced
juice of ½ lemon
115g/4oz/4 cups red salad leaves, such
  as lollo rosso, oakleaf and radicchio
200g/7oz cooked beetroot (beets), peeled
  and sliced

For the dressing
30ml/2 tbsp olive oil
15ml/1 tbsp walnut oil
15ml/1 tbsp cider vinegar
ground black pepper

1 Toast the almonds in a dry frying pan for 2–3 minutes until golden brown.

2 Meanwhile, make the dressing. Put the olive and walnut oils, cider vinegar and ground black pepper in a bowl or screw-top jar. Stir or shake thoroughly to combine the ingredients.

3 Toss the diced apples in lemon juice to prevent them browning, then place in a large bowl and add the salad leaves and beetroot.

4 Pour over the dressing and toss gently. Scatter the toasted almonds over the dressed salad and serve.

Cook's tip
If using raw beetroot, it can be cooked by baking in a little water in a covered dish, or it can be simmered for about 1½ hours in boiling water. Trim the stalks, but don't cut away the root or peel it – or the red colour will bleed away.

Energy 191Kcal/793kJ; Protein 4.1g; Carbohydrate 9.5g, of which sugars 8.8g; Fat 15.5g, of which saturates 1.6g; Cholesterol 0mg; Calcium 54mg; Fibre 2.7g; Sodium 58mg.

Marinated courgette and flageolet bean salad

Serve this healthy salad as a light lunch or as an accompaniment to fish or chicken dishes. It has a wonderful bright green colour and is perfect for a summer lunch.

Serves 4

2 courgettes (zucchini), halved lengthways
    and sliced
400g/14oz can flageolet or cannellini beans,
    drained and rinsed
45ml/3 tbsp garlic-infused olive oil
grated rind and juice of 1 lemon
30ml/2 tbsp fresh basil and mint, chopped
ground black pepper

1 Cook the sliced courgettes in a large pan of lightly salted boiling water for 2–3 minutes, or until just tender. Drain well in a colander and refresh under cold running water.

2 Transfer the drained courgettes into a bowl with the beans and stir in the oil, lemon rind and juice and pepper, to season. Cover and chill for 30 minutes. Add the chopped herbs and toss together just before serving.

Energy 183Kcal/766kJ; Protein 7.8g; Carbohydrate 18.7g, of which sugars 4.5g; Fat 9.1g, of which saturates 1.3g; Cholesterol 0mg; Calcium 84mg; Fibre 6.7g; Sodium 391mg.

Butter bean, tomato and red onion salad

Make good use of canned beans in a simple side salad. Serve as an accompaniment to a main dish, or serve several salads together for a healthy main meal.

Serves 4

2 x 400g/14oz cans butter (lima) beans, rinsed and drained
4 plum tomatoes, roughly chopped
1 red onion, thinly sliced
45ml/3 tbsp herb-infused olive oil
ground black pepper

1 Mix together the beans, tomatoes and onion in a large bowl. Season with ground black pepper to taste, and stir in the oil.

2 Cover the bowl with clear film (plastic wrap) and chill in the refrigerator for 20 minutes before serving.

Energy 251Kcal/1055kJ; Protein 12.7g; Carbohydrate 30.3g, of which sugars 6.2g; Fat 9.6g, of which saturates 1.5g; Cholesterol 0mg; Calcium 41mg; Fibre 10.4g; Sodium 850mg.

delicious fruit salads

Although most desserts should be avoided during a weekend detox, fruit salads are allowed since they provide a great opportunity to pack plenty of vitamins into your diet. Vary the types of fruit that you use so that you get the maximum range of vitamins and minerals, and avoid adding extra sugar if possible; use honey instead.

Fresh fruit salad

A healthy diet should include plenty of fresh fruit, and the wide variety available throughout the seasons means that it's always easy to put together a delicious combination of fruit for a healthy dessert or snack. Fruit salads are especially beneficial during a detox regime, as fruit helps to eliminate toxins. This simple version could also be enjoyed for breakfast.

Serves 4

16–20 strawberries
2 peaches
2 oranges
2 eating apples
30ml/2 tbsp lemon juice
15–30ml/1–2 tbsp orange flower
   water (optional)
a few fresh mint leaves, to decorate

Variations
There are no rules with this fruit salad, and you could add any other fruit that you like, such as bananas and grapes.

1 Hull the strawberries and cut them in half. Put the peaches in a bowl, pour boiling water over them and leave them to stand for 1 minute.

2 Remove from the water, using a slotted spoon. Peel, then cut the flesh into thick slices. Discard the stones (pits).

3 Peel the oranges, removing all the pith, and segment, catching any juice in a small bowl. Peel, core and chop the apples. Place all the fruit in a large serving bowl.

4 Combine the lemon juice, orange flower water, if using, and any reserved orange juice. Pour the fruit juice mixture over the salad and serve decorated with a few fresh mint leaves.

Health benefits
Fruit cleanses and rejuvenates the body, as well as providing minerals, vitamins and fibre.

Dried fruit salad

This wonderful combination of fresh and dried fruit makes an excellent detox dessert. Both types are packed with nutrients and will provide plenty of energy. The dried selection includes apricots and peaches, and the fresh selection includes pear, apple, orange, blackberries and raspberries, but you can ring the changes with your own favourite combination.

Serves 4

115g/4oz/½ cup dried apricots
115g/4oz/½ cup dried peaches
1 pear
1 apple
1 orange
50g/2oz/½ cup blackberries
1 cinnamon stick
45ml/3 tbsp clear unblended honey
30ml/2 tbsp lemon juice
50g/2oz/½ cup raspberries

1 Place the apricots and peaches in a bowl and cover with water. Leave to soak for 1–2 hours or overnight in the refrigerator until plump, then drain. Cut the soaked fruit into equal size pieces with a sharp knife.

2 Peel and core the pear and apple and cut into cubes. Peel the orange with a sharp knife, removing all the pith, and cut into wedges. Place all the prepared fruit in a large pan with the blackberries.

3 Add 600ml/1 pint/2½ cups water, the cinnamon and honey to the pan and bring to the boil.

4 Cover and simmer very gently for 10–12 minutes, then remove the pan from the heat. Stir in the lemon juice and raspberries. Allow the mixture to cool, then pour into a bowl. Cover and chill in the refrigerator for about 1 hour before serving.

Cook's tips
• Ideally, choose unsulphured dried fruit. Much dried fruit is treated with sulphur-based preservatives to prevent discoloration and enhance the colour, but it is best avoided, especially by those with asthma.
• Avoid ready-to-eat dried fruit, as it contains lots of preservatives.

Top: Energy 78Kcal/331kJ; Protein 2.1g; Carbohydrate 18g, of which sugars 18g; Fat 0.2g, of which saturates 0g; Cholesterol 0mg; Calcium 50mg; Fibre 3.5g; Sodium 8mg.
Above: Energy 162Kcal/689kJ; Protein 3.1g; Carbohydrate 38.6g, of which sugars 38.6g; Fat 0.5g, of which saturates 0g; Cholesterol 0mg; Calcium 70mg; Fibre 5.9g; Sodium 13mg.

Fresh fruit with mango coulis

A flavourful fruit sauce, or coulis, is easy to prepare and ideal for transforming a simple fruit salad into something special. Making a coulis also provides an opportunity for adding extra fruit to this dessert. Mangoes make a luscious coulis, but other soft fruits, such as raspberries, strawberries or peaches, would make good alternatives.

Serves 4–6

1 large ripe mango, peeled, stoned and chopped
rind of 1 orange
juice of 3 oranges
caster (superfine) sugar, to taste
2 peaches
2 nectarines
1 small mango, peeled
2 plums
1 pear or ½ small melon
juice of 1 lemon
50g/2oz/2 heaped tbsp wild
    strawberries (optional)
50g/2oz/2 heaped tbsp raspberries
50g/2oz/2 heaped tbsp blueberries
small fresh mint sprigs, to decorate

1 In a food processor fitted with a metal blade, blend the chopped flesh of the large mango until smooth. Add the orange rind and juice and a little sugar to taste and process again until very smooth. Press through a sieve (strainer) into a bowl and chill.

2 Slice and stone the peaches, nectarines, small mango and plums. Quarter the pear and remove the core or, if using, slice the melon thinly and remove the skin.

3 Place the sliced fruits on a large plate, sprinkle with the lemon juice and chill, covered with clear film (plastic wrap), for up to 3 hours. (Some fruits discolour if cut too far ahead of time.)

4 To serve, arrange the sliced fruits on serving plates, spoon the berries on top, drizzle with a little mango coulis and decorate with mint sprigs. Serve the remaining coulis separately.

Cook's tip
Ideally choose unwaxed or organic citrus fruit, if you are going to be using the rind. If they are not unwaxed, wash the fruit thoroughly before using, because the waxes contain fungicide.

Energy 82Kcal/351kJ; Protein 1.9g; Carbohydrate 19.2g, of which sugars 19.1g; Fat 0.3g, of which saturates 0.1g; Cholesterol 0mg; Calcium 22mg; Fibre 3.3g; Sodium 5mg.

Exotic fruit platter with ginger

Pineapple, papaya, melon and pomegranates offer an impressive range of detoxifying qualities. There is no need to save this refreshing platter for dessert. Fruit prepared in this way is delicious as an energy-boosting snack or breakfast during a detox. Serve on its own or with some low-fat probiotic yogurt. Omit the ground ginger, if you prefer.

Serves 4–6

1 pineapple
2 papayas
1 melon
juice of 2 limes
2 pomegranates
ground ginger, to taste
sprigs of mint, to decorate

1 Peel the pineapple. Remove the core, then cut the flesh lengthways into thin wedges. Peel the papayas, cut them in half, remove the seeds, then slice into thin wedges.

2 Halve the melon and remove the seeds from the middle. Cut into thin wedges and remove the skin.

Health benefits
Fresh mint has traditionally been used as a cure for indigestion and is also effective in stimulating and cleansing the system.

Variation
The selection of fruit can be varied. Apples and bananas make a simple salad, or guavas and mangoes a more exotic combination. Rather than using ginger, simply season with freshly ground black pepper.

3 Arrange the fruit on six individual plates and sprinkle with the lime juice. Cut the pomegranates in half and scoop out the seeds, discarding any pith. Scatter the seeds over the fruit. Serve, sprinkled with a little ginger to taste, and a few sprigs of mint.

Energy 91Kcal/389kJ; Protein 1.2g; Carbohydrate 22.1g, of which sugars 22.1g; Fat 0.4g, of which saturates 0g; Cholesterol 0mg; Calcium 48mg; Fibre 3.4g; Sodium 32mg.

Index

Acknowledgements

Photographers: Karl Adamson; Edward Allwright; Peter Anderson; David Armstrong; Tim Auty; Steve Baxter; Martin Brigdale; Nicky Dowey; James Duncan; Gus Filgate; Ian Garlick; Michelle Garrett; John Heseltine; Amanda Heywood; Tim Hill; Janine Hosegood; Dave King; Don Last; William Lingwood; Patrick McLeavey; Michael Michaels; Steve Moss; Thomas Odulate; Peter Reilly; Craig Robertson; Bridget Sargeson; Simon Smith; Sam Stowell.

Recipe writers: Pepita Aris; Catherine Atkinson; Stephanie Barker; Ghillie Başan; Judy Bastyra; Susannah Blake; Angela Boggiano; Georgina Campbell; Carla Capalbo; Lesley Chamberlain; Maxine Clarke; Carole Clements; Trish Davies; Roz Denny; Patrizia Diemling; Stephanie Donaldson; Matthew Drennan; Sarah Edmonds; Steve England; Joanna Farrow; Rafi Fernandez; Jenni Fleetwood; Christine France; Silvana Franco; Sarah Gates; Shirley Gill; Brian Glover; Nicola Graimes; Rosamund Grant; Carole Handslip; Rebekah Hassan; Shehzaid Husain; Christine Ingram; Becky Johnson; Soheila Kimberley; Lucy Knox; Elizabeth Lambert Ortiz; Ruby Le Bois; Patricia Lousada; Gilly Love; Lesley Mackey; Norma MacMillan; Sue Maggs; Kathy Man; Sally Mansfield; Elizabeth Martin; Maggie Mayhew; Sarah Maxwell; Norma Miller; Jane Milton; Sallie Morris; Janice Murfitt; Annie Nichols; Angela Nilsen; Suzannah Olivier; Maggie Pannell; Louise Pickford; Marion Price; Keith Richmond; Rena Salaman; Anne Sheasby; Marlena Spieler; Liz Trigg; Christopher Trotter; Linda Tubby; Hilaire Walden; Laura Washburn; Biddy White Lennon; Kate Whiteman; Judy Williams; Carol Wilson; Elizabeth Wolf-Cohen; Jeni Wright.

Food stylists and home economists: Alison Austin; Eliza Baird; Alex Barker; Shannon Beare; Julie Beresford; Madeleine Brehaut; Sascha Brodie; Jacqueline Clarke; Frances Cleary; Stephanie England; Tessa Evelegh; Marilyn Forbes; Annabel Ford; Nicola Fowler; Michelle Garrett; Hilary Guy; Jo Harris; Jane Hartshorn; Katherine Hawkins; Amanda Heywood; Cara Hobday; Claire Hunt; Kate Jay; Jill Jones; Maria Kelly; Clare Lewis; Sara Lewis; Lucy McKelvie; Marion McLornan; Wendy Lee; Blake Minton; Emma Patmore; Marion Price; Kirsty Rawlings; Bridget Sargeson; Jennie Shapter; Joy Skipper; Jane Stephenson; Carol Tenant; Helen Trent; Linda Tubby; Sunil Vijayakar; Stuart Walton; Sophie Wheeler; Stephen Wheeler; Judy Williams.